Upwards

Printed in the United States of America

First Printing 2017

ISBN- 978-1541098176

Aaron Hunnel
Appleton, WI 54914

pressplay@aaronhunnel.com

www.aaronhunnel.com

Special discounts are available on quantity purchases by corporations, associations, and others. For details, contact Aaron at the email address or website above.

Upwards

*Maximize Life with Positivity,
Passion and Purpose*

Written by Aaron Hunnel

To my wife, Marissa, who always sees the best in me.

Contents

Introduction

Gratitude can be one of the greatest blessings we choose to experience. It costs very little, and yet, at the same time, invigorates our mind, our bodies and our soul. We'll get more into that as you read further; but, first, I want to know, "How is your life unfolding at this present moment?" Are you achieving all that you desire? Do you feel alive and free or full of shame and discontent? Does it feel like each morning you wake up ready to tackle the day, or is life unraveling, spiraling downward? Are you living in a state consciousness, of presence and peace, or do you feel stuck doing the same old things and getting the same old results? No matter how you currently feel, or where you may be in your life, I'd like to invite you to keep pushing through. The fact that you woke up this morning despite all of the adversity you've faced in life, truly testifies your strength. You have breath. You have a heart which beats. You are blessed with the most amazing gift. The gift of life. I want this book to be about you and your path to achieving all that you've always wanted for yourself: happiness, health, financial freedom, whatever that may be, Know that you are an amazing individual with a unique story—so unique that your experiences are unlike anyone else's ever! Out of an estimated 108

1

billion people that have ever lived, the unfolding of your life has never occurred before. You are the only you.

By the time you finish reading this book, I want you to have the understanding, attitude, hope, and belief that you are capable of achieving whatever you want in this life. Writing this book testifies that. My past is full of shame. I experienced brokenness and created deep emotional wounds for myself, friends and family. I failed time and time again, lost my way and eventually hit rock bottom.

I continued this downward spiral until one day, I had this epiphany. Things in life didn't happen to me, but rather for me. I realized I had struggled, battled and persevered to overcome something quite extraordinary. While deployed in Iraq, I completed the Boston Marathon satellite race. If you've never heard of a marathon, it's a 26.2 mile race where people run... for fun! I remember when my friend, April, originally asked me if I wanted to take on this challenge: "Are you nuts?"

I said. "Running is not something I intend to do for fun. Especially for that long."

I didn't even know how long a marathon was when she asked. I just knew it was longer than I'd ever care to run. Then she responded, almost as if she knew it would be the tipping point to capturing my buy-in, "They give you a t-shirt and a medal at the end!"

I didn't need to hear anything else. "A coveted Boston Marathon medal and t-shirt!" I said. "Sign me up!"

As I let this commitment sink in, I started to realize what I had just gotten myself into. I had made a choice to do something that I had no idea how to do. Because I was in the Army, I knew how to run two miles (which is required for our annual fitness test), but I had no clue what to do after that. So I did what any logical person would do: I started winging it as best I could.

Now it is important to note that, while I continue to tell my story, all of this directly relates to the learning that will occur throughout this book. Whether you are a runner or not, the applications for life and all that I believe to be true about complete and transformational behavior change begins with this story. So runner, jumper, walker, roller, driver, or however you get from place to place, it will make sense as you continue reading. Running—or life for that matter—requires two things: First, you need the right stuff. You need the right equipment such as running shoes, polyester socks and clothing, and a proper diet. With those things, you can start your journey towards whatever distance you're willing to take on. Second, you need action. What good is the right equipment if it never gets used? Answer– none! You must take action and prepare for any race that you wish to accomplish. Such is life. You need the right equipment in life to help support yourself to achieve all that you want. To paraphrase Albert Einstein, to succeed in life, you can't just keep doing the same things over and over and expect things to change. You must take action once you have the right equipment and put into practice exactly what you want to achieve.

My hope is that this book becomes a tool that you can use for your life. One filled with positivity, passion, and purpose.

Positivity, passion, and purpose comprise the most useful tools one can use in life. They are the pillars that help to support all that you want for yourself. We'll explore these pillars more in–depth as you continue reading. To set the tone for what you're about to experience, allow me to give you a glimpse into why I believe in the necessity of these pillars.

Positivity:

An intentionally positive attitude finds subtle blessings in many day-to-day circumstances others might not appreciate. Living with positivity yields increased optimism, resiliency, and hope.

Passion:

Passion helps you find what you love and then continue to do it. When younger, many of us dreamed of becoming a policeman, firefighter, astronaut, doctor, or veterinarian. Many of us still have dreams of living our greatest life. Finding your passion can help align those dreams and make them a reality.

Purpose:

Last, but definitely not least, is purpose. "What is my reason for living? What can I contribute to humanity? What will make me feel alive every single day?" Such questions help clarify your purpose during this short time on earth. Knowing who you are and living according to your purpose and values transcends mediocrity, hopelessness, and shame.

What good are positivity, passion, and purpose without action? What good is it to know how to be happy if you don't take action? What good is it to know your passion, but never take a chance to put it into practice? What good is purpose with no intention to use it to create a better life for humanity, or even for yourself?

Action is necessary for your life to take flight and lift you above your circumstances, your environment, your fears, and your regrets. Newton's third law of motion states that for every action, there is an equal and opposite reaction. Metaphorically speaking, if we put good out into the world, good is what we receive. If we put bad out into the world, bad is what we receive. In layman's terms, it's about reaping what you sow; also known as karma.

You receive opportunities at many divergences in your life to take action and choose the things important to you. You are aware of some, while others pass by you unnoticed. As long as you continuously pursue a life of positivity, passion, and purpose, you see and seize these opportunities, taking action and creating abundance in your life. You will reap as you sow.

Most people miss opportunities because they fail to act. They weigh the risk, become discouraged by fear, and make excuses. Consequently, they miss opportunities. I've learned that those who achieved a successful life by starting a business, finding happiness, or changing the world (I say this because success is relative and different for everyone), is that they take risks. They have courage and eliminate excuses. Doing the same will increase your trajectory in life.

To move upwards, you must climb, persevere, and keep moving forward. It's like scaling a mountain. You keep moving towards the summit. It's hard, challenging, and scary. But the further you climb, you notice that your perspective changes. You can now see for miles around and the view is breathtaking. Moving upwards empowers you to have the perspective to see the beauty around you. As you come to appreciate what you see, you start to change what you believe. You realize that you are capable of more than you ever imagined. You see things more clearly than ever. You feel a renewed sense of energy, motivation, and momentum. Everything about you seems elevated and lifted.

This book, which I hope you consider a journey, aims to help you discover the steps necessary for you to go after your dreams, live up to your potential, and generate momentum in life. Wherever you are, understand that, although I might not know you, I know you are capable of achieving something great. Whatever you think your limits are, I want you to know that they are exponentially higher.

Get ready, because we're going to stretch, bend, and expand your limits, your thinking, and your success. We're moving upwards, together.

Chapter 1:
Positivity

Have you ever had an experience so profound that you can't help but recall it throughout your life as a teaching and reflecting point? Such an experience may have shaped your thinking, gave you valuable perspective, or made you feel special. I recall such an experience when I was ten years old during what I believe to be the best Christmas ever.

It was a chilly, overcast day in southwest Missouri on December 23rd. We lived in a small, double-wide mobile home in front of a tree line that separated our yard from an open field. We had two baby trees in the front yard and one large walnut tree between our home and the church next door. I loved that walnut tree. It kept me busy throughout the year. I loved to climb it during the summer. Its branches took me up, up, and up, so I could see over our home and down the street. One particular branch extended long and low to the ground, perfect for swinging and bouncing upon. When I hung from the end of the branch, my feet barely touching the ground, I felt like I could jump a mile in the sky. That tree also helped me make the little league baseball team. When the walnuts dropped from the tree and scatter over the ground, you had to watch where you were walking so you didn't step on one and roll an ankle. I would pick up walnuts, one by one, and hurl them at the tree trunk. Sometimes I would pretend like I was a major league pitcher in game seven of the World Series: two outs, full count, bases loaded. We'd be up by one run and the next pitch would decide if we won or lost the Word Series. I'd sling that fastball (or fast walnut) right at that tree for strike three, and almost always win the World Series. Those walnuts fueled the fire of my imagination.

They weren't just for throwing, though. My family and I collected the walnuts and turned them in for money. We spent hours walking around with brown paper bags, picking up the walnuts and placing them in bags.

Walnuts produce a smelly residue that turns your hands to a green color when you handle them. The sour stench requires lots of soap and hand scrubbing to get rid of the smell. My family needed the money from those walnuts.

Six of us lived in that trailer then: my mom and dad, two sisters, one brother, me, and another brother on the way. My dad served as pastor for the church next door. It was a typical small church in a small town. The white paint on the outside was extremely weathered, old and peeling. The inside reminded me of a historical museum and smelled of mothballs—stale, old, antique. My dad earned $100 a week pastoring that church. He was a very busy man trying to provide for his family. He picked many jobs up just to try to make ends meet. He worked all the time. He visited people all the time. I didn't see him very much, except on Sundays. My mom stayed at home with all of us children. Our large family in this trailer home made us feel sardines packed in a can.

I didn't care, though. I loved my family. On December 23rd, my parents brought my brothers and sisters together into the living room and sat us down on the couch. Our Christmas tree was off to our right, the string of lights flashing to the beat of Silent Night, which played on the little speaker built into the cord. The quality of the speaker made the song sound techno. I returned my attention to my mom and dad. They looked discouraged. Heads were down. No smiling—which was strange, because they were both happy people.

"What is it?" I asked.

"We're very sorry to tell you kids this, but finances aren't looking good this year and we're not going to be able to buy Christmas presents."

I wondered what that meant. Sure, I realized we were poor, but were we really that poor? I felt ashamed. Almost as quickly as I came to that realization, my mind snapped back to the conscious point of realizing what truly mattered. That, of course, was my family. I was disappointed, not by the fact that my parents couldn't afford presents, but because they were struggling. As much as they wanted to give us something tangible for the season when it was expected to give a gift, they could not. We were a family of six—soon to be seven—and we had the greatest gifts of all: each other.

Life has a funny way of working out sometimes, even when you least expect it. When you look past all the pain and suffering, there is goodness, kindness and hope.

The day after my parents broke the news a white van pulled into the driveway. It was old and a little rusted. The tires were worn from what seemed like years and years of use and the onset of rust where the body met the frame. Two men jumped out, one a bit older than the other. He had white hair and a mustache. He wore blue jeans and boots with a collared flannel shirt and rolled-up sleeves. The other man had short, black hair and a scruffy beard. He wore jeans also, coupled with a pair of tennis shoes and a white t–shirt. They slowly made their way up to the door. My dad greeted them with a beaming smile. They shook hands as my dad followed them to the truck.

"What is going on here?" I thought to myself.

The vantage point of the living room window to the back of the truck blocked me and my siblings from the mystery of what lay inside that truck. What made Dad so happy? All three men came out from behind the truck with boxes in their arms— boxes wrapped with paper in the most magnificent colors. I leapt from the couch and quickly made my way to the door and flung it open. There stood the two men and my father.

The elder man looked down at me, his eyes filled with joy and happiness. In a very deep and rustic voice, he said, "Merry Christmas."

That man, along with his church, had adopted us as a family and they brought presents for me and my siblings. As they unloaded the truck, I became curious how many presents were under that tree.

One... two... I kept counting.

Thirty-one... thrity-two. Wow, thirty-two presents so far. And yet they kept coming. By the time the men had unloaded all of those presents, I counted forty-four packages.

"Are you kidding me?" I thought. "Forty-four presents!"

As I looked at each package individually, I read the names on the packages. William, Kristin, Sarah, Aaron. I searched the pile for my parents' names.

"Where were their presents?" I thought. "They have to be here somewhere."

Nothing. All that stood there were presents for the kids.

"What about you guys?" I asked my parents. "How come you don't get any?"

My inexperience in life brought me to this question. I just couldn't fathom how I would get so much, yet my parents received nothing.

"Don't worry," my parents responded. "Your happiness is the only gift we need."

That Christmas, I went from having no presents to having eleven. I realized three valuable lessons from that experience.

First, there are gifts all around us if we intentionally seek them. Life will present you with adverse experiences that make you question your strength, your mental fortitude, your value, or your self–worth. When adversity comes, you can look at it from two different perspectives. From one perspective, you can see this as a confirmation of who you are. It defines you and what you are capable of achieving in life. For example, I could have seen the fact that I had no presents as confirmation of my family's financial troubles. I could have criticized my parents for the lifestyle I had. I could have resented other kids who were so fortunate as to receive gifts. What would this type of thinking achieve? To me, very little. From the other perspective, you can see this experience as is something that carries value. It does not define you, rather it refines you. I chose to focus on something I believed carried more value. Sure, I wanted presents: what kid doesn't? But I soon came to realize that if my desire for presents trumped my desire for love (in this case from and for my family), then I would miss out on all that truly mattered. By choosing to use the perspective of love, I was better able to handle the situation and avoid possible contamination from fear, anger, and shame.

The second lesson I learned from receiving gifts as an adopted family was that people are amazing creatures. We are full of love, compassion, joy, and peace. These are some of the purest forms of human emotion, most of which enable the greatest human experience. And when these are present in life, it drives out anger, greed, selfishness and pride. In the same way that darkness cannot exist where there is light, fear cannot exist where there is love. Anger cannot exist where there is joy. Greed cannot exist where there is compassion. Pride cannot exist where there is peace. Each of these emotions rests within us. The emotion that manifests in our life, into our consciousness, or even into our sub-consciousness, is the one that we choose. When that church and those men displayed these loving acts, it drove out any feelings of fear, doubt, and inadequacy. The positive emotions I felt from their kindness made me realize the true nature of the human spirit. I realized at this point—just ten years old—that life was about giving more than you take. It was about using your strengths, talents, and treasures to make someone else's day. The more good you put out into the world, the more good you get.

The final lesson I learned from that experience was that you never know how long a decision or a choice will influence not only you but also the world around you. That church and those men likely had no clue how big of a role their kindness played in my life. Some years later, I can still recall the details of that day. Think back to an experience that was so profound in your life that you can recall it specifically today. Can you remember what you saw? What you heard? What you smelled? Our brain's capacity to collect and retain certain information and experiences based on the different senses, both physical and metaphysical— because spiritual enlightenment contributes to the experience of one's existence— influences the choices we make and eventually who we become. That experience when I was ten, along with many other experiences in my life, is what made me realize how important positive emotion is to the human mind, body, and spirit.

By no means has my life always been positive. I've made poor choices, but this contrast in experiences provided me with the knowledge to make a choice to be better. Furthermore, it is in those tough times that I now see it was necessary for me to struggle so that I could take all that I learned and use it to shape my life. I'm sure you've experienced a tough time in your life as well. One way that you can overcome challenges in life is to make the choice to give.

Positivity is not just a feeling, it is an experience, one that I feel is fundamental in our lives. There is a unique relationship that exists when you give; you can give your time, your money, your heart, your love. What's interesting about this relationship is that when you give, you get. Let me say that again, because I think it's extremely important: When you give, you get.

This is not a selfish idea, but rather an enlightened idea. When you give something of yourself, there are many people who benefit: The person who received your gift, the person giving the gift, and anyone who witnessed the gift giving. They all benefit, but for different reasons. Think about when someone was kind to you. Maybe that person bought you a cup of coffee. Maybe he or she took time out of his or her busy day to teach you a skill. The brain processes this kindness in a way that can improve mood and resiliency. The idea is that we are innately wired to be kind to people. When we choose to be aggressive or act out of anger towards others, we resist our very nature.

Our species, the human race, was meant to survive together. This concept is not just psychological or spiritual, it's also physiological. Kindness triggers a chemical response in our brain. Dopamine, a neurotransmitter that acts as the reward system in our brain, makes us feel good when we give, receive, or witness the giving. If you've ever gotten a great deal on a pair of pants, won the lottery, or completed a goal, dopamine is the chemical that makes you feel rewarded. And when you feel rewarded, you're more likely to make that choice again. Think about that the next time you walk into a department store and find the piece of clothing you want and it's on sale. You purchase it and feel like a million bucks! Guess where you might be more inclined to shop the next time you need a new article of clothing? My guess is, you would likely go back to the place that made you feel like a winner. Performing acts of kindness can make us feel rewarded. The more we do it, the more ingrained of a behavior it becomes in our lives. When your behavior regularly includes acts of kindness, it can lead to greater happiness and total well-being.

Consider oxytocin, also known as the love hormone, which is secreted during acts of kindness (It's also the chemical that compels mothers to love their babies after giving birth).

This hormone, which is also believed to regulate empathy—putting yourself in someone else's shoes—acts as a bridge to make people feel connected and loved. It is one of the foundations of friendship. When you perform an act of kindness, oxytocin is secreted for the person giving the gift, the person receiving the gift, and any bystanders who witness the gift giving. Simply put, acts of kindness bring people together.

Now dopamine and oxytocin don't just make

people feel rewarded and connected, they also influence the circulatory system. Let's say, for example, you perform an act of kindness and you get this sensation of reward and connection with the person you gave your money or time to. Dopamine and oxytocin play a role in vasodilation, which expands blood vessels and reduces blood pressure. The number one disease in the United States is heart disease, with high blood pressure being a risk factor for heart disease. So essentially, performing an act of kindness is good for mood, relationships, and health. These are the gifts that you receive for performing acts of kindness. Like I said earlier, these are not selfish gifts; rather they are gifts that are given in return for your giving. As you continue to give, you will continue to receive. The more you receive, not just physically, but mentally and spiritually, the more abundance you create in your life.

Hermes Trismegistus once said, "As above, so below, as within, so without." That means giving isn't something you do, but rather something you become, something you are. If you give, you are a giver, and the universe gives back to you. So, knowing this, should acts of kindness be random? Or rather, should they be intentional? To me, a random act of kindness is explicitly what the phrase states: "random." If something is random, then it holds no definite pattern or reason. It merely exists or comes about at the time of occurrence. I think that this is a big miss for humanity. Acts of kindness should be intentional. They should embody our values, our beliefs, and our culture. They should be made intentionally with love. They should be made intentionally with service.

Think about everything in life which competes for your time and attention. Think about the people who might inflict deep emotional wounds and give only negative perspective. Consider how you react when things happen outside your control. The world has experienced negativity, fear and pain throughout its history. People fear what they can't control. However, once negativity enters your thinking, you lose the actual control you once sought. History will continue to repeat this negative, habitual thinking because we are programmed to seek control. Therefore, since we seek control, fear will always be present. Negativity exists in that fear, and since negativity exists, control cannot be fully achieved. We find ourselves in a viscous cycling chasing to control something that doesn't exist. Fear fuels negativity and pessimism in our life. The only way to combat these negative emotions is not to reduce them, but to overcome them. Now I'm not saying that acts of kindness will rid the world of fear or control hate, but it will positively change your life and the lives of others. Negativity is easy. Acting out of fear, anger or hate is easy. It takes self-management and great personal awareness and acceptance to make the choice to act out of love.

Research supports that it is easier to move from a positive emotional state to a negative emotional state than it is to move from a negative emotional state to a positive emotional state. Think about how you felt the last time someone did something you disagreed with or took advantage of you; or perhaps, maybe you just turned on the news. It's extremely easy to see the bad in things. It's easy to feel bad as an initial response. It's easy to be afraid and let fear hijack our emotions and decisions. But, just as the wise Jedi knight, Yoda, explains to young Anakin Skywalker, the future Darth Vader, "Fear leads to anger. Anger leads to hate. Hate leads to suffering." If we act out of fear, then we are likely to suffer. But if we act out of love, we are likely to succeed.

Acting out of love is difficult. But only at first, because the more you do it, the more you practice, the better it gets. Barbara Fredrickson, a researcher from the University of North Carolina, states that, because negativity carries such a heavy weight, we must work almost three times as hard to incorporate positive experiences into our lives. She calls this the positivity/negativity ratio. For every negative emotion or experience you have, you need three positive emotions or experiences to offset the impact. Those who achieve at least this ratio are considered to be thriving in life. Here's a startling fact Fredrickson mentions: "[Eighty] percent of people fail to meet this ratio." Knowing this, shouldn't we intentionally incorporate more positivity into our lives? The answer is yes.

Positivity, as I've pointed out, is good for people. It helps us overcome the constructs of negative thinking, it can influence good health, and it helps us build relationships. So, what can you do? First, you must be intentional behind incorporating more kindness into your life. This doesn't have to be complicated. Just remember, the more you do it, the easier it gets, and the more it becomes a part of you.

Following are some simple ways to incorporate more intentional acts of kindness into your life:

Hold the door for people: If you see someone within five seconds of going through the same door as you, then hold it for him or her. Whether you are walking into work, the grocery store, or a restaurant, hold the door. If you see a group of people coming, then hold it for the entire group. Most will appreciate the gesture and thank you. All get to experience the positive light that pours from you to them.

Mind your manners: Say, "thank you," "please," and "you're welcome." Stay away from yeah, sure, ummhmm, or other words that sound insincere. Words are extremely powerful: they can build or break relationships. They can tell stories and convey emotions. Thank-you, please, and you're welcome are some basic words that must be part of your vocabulary. I used to go to a certain Indian restaurant just because I loved being served by a particular waiter. He understood the power of words and articulated his kindness well. Every time I said thanks or thank-you, he would respond with, "You're welcome," not "Sure," not a downward head nod, not quick "ummhmm," but a clear and well–articulated, "You're welcome." I was so fascinated by his consistency that I would even test it by saying thanks as often as I could. His response was always, "You're welcome." His intentional speaking of those words every time moved me. It made me consider how I showed appreciation or acknowledgment in my own life. Although these are basic words, sometimes we have to get back to the basics and work on fundamentals to gain the momentum to incorporate more positivity into our lives. Remember that three-to-one ratio? Imagine using this in the first example above where you hold the door for a group of people and each one thanks you. Try to you say "you're welcome" to each person that shows gratitude. This way it becomes more personalized.

Bring a snack or coffee to your next team meeting: The other day a colleague offered to buy me a coffee. My current organization offers free coffee—note that the coffee there is horrible, so this gesture required two things. First, she would have to go offsite to purchase this coffee. Second, she would have to buy it. So, it requires her time and money. I felt extremely thankful and appreciative.

Actively listen when someone talks to you: Ask questions, smile, and nod your head to show that you are listening. Many of us listen to respond, rather than to understand. People want to be heard. People need to be heard. Listening with a spirit of service and out of love is an act of kindness that is too often overlooked. If you want to make someone feel empowered, listen to them!

Smile: Smiling is the universal language of happiness. It is also the most explicit form of consciousness because it conveys the positive internal emotions one feels and outwardly projects those emotions. Another unique quality of the smile is its ability to render smiles from others. When someone smiles at another individual, the response is often a smile. Children set a fine example of how often we should smile. According to Robert Provine, children smile an average of three hundred plus times per day; adults, on the other hand, smile fewer than twenty. So, give someone your smile. Don't worry, they won't keep it. They'll give it right back.

Practice gratitude: Send someone a thank-you letter or email. Think about someone who had a positive influence in your life and let them know how much they mean to you. It can be a friend or family member, but it doesn't have to stop there. You can reach out to authors, musicians, speakers, anyone. The digital age has made access to people and personal connection very easy. I've written a couple of authors, thought leaders, and musicians. It's fun to receive a response from a person whose book you read. Remember, it's the intention behind the action and not the response you may receive that is important. You shouldn't send this letter or message with the intention of receiving a response. Just the fact that you are sending it shows how much you appreciate that person. You may get a response; then again, you may not. Either outcome is okay. The value is in the effort you put into the kindness.

Do you want to throw a little randomness into your kindness? Here's how you can do it. Print out five pieces of paper with an inspirational message on them. It can be a quote or a short message. Whatever it is, make sure that it has a positive vibe. Carry these pieces of paper with you and randomly assign when you will give each piece of paper out. For example, you could say, I'm going to give a message to the first person I see at work, getting gas, walking on the sidewalk, at the gym. The list goes on. You don't have to tell them your name, just politely say that you have a message that you'd like to give them. Thank them for accepting, and go about your day. You could get really creative with this if you want and write down these messages on sticky notes. Then you don't even have to wait to find someone; you could go into stealth mode and just leave them secretly for people to find.

Give someone a compliment: Sometimes we get so preoccupied with our automatic and unconscious way of living that we forget to notice the people around us. Pay attention to the next time you are at the office, out in public, wherever. Count how many people acknowledge you. Although this isn't always the case, most often you'll find, especially in organizations or communities with poor culture, climate, or cohesiveness, that people just entirely avoid others when they walk by. This exercise isn't to pass judgment, but rather to increase awareness of how we sometimes live on autopilot without even knowing that we do so. We get so preoccupied with the past or future that we forget to live in the moment, the present.

A simple compliment can go a very long way. Keep it simple so the person does not becomes self-conscious. This means that you should avoid mentioning weight and clothes. Doing so might make the other person feel a little awkward, as though you're judging them. People like to feel valued. In fact, we perform better when we are valued by the people, organizations, and communities of which we are part. If you are a leader or want to show someone you care for them, then compliments must be a constant part of your interaction. Failure to provide feedback can create an extreme lack of clarity for how one performs or lives their life.

- "I appreciate everything you are doing'"

- "I've noticed how hard you've been working."

- "I value and appreciate all that you are and all that you want to become." "You are awesome."

These statements are simple, yet powerful.

You've probably realized that all of these intentional acts of kindness are relatively inexpensive and don't take a lot of time. That's the point. All of this is extremely simple, yet we often fail to make the conscious choice to be kind to others. Kindness can lead to many positive emotions. Positive emotions are great experiences which enable us to be fully alive. You weren't meant to live a life full of anger and frustration, fear and shame, pain and guilt. Life was meant to be abundant; sometimes we have to shake off the cobwebs of our own thinking and look deep into what drives our emotions, our beliefs, our attitudes, our choices, and our lives.

Living with positivity is the first pillar in what I believe is necessary to fully function at our optimal potential and attract the right types of opportunities and people into our lives to help us create more momentum. Experiencing positive emotions results in happiness. Rather than trying to make yourself happy through fulfillment of superficial wants and desires, focus on increasing your positive emotions through conscious thinking. Superficial wants and desires will often leave you unfulfilled and result in a short, but inauthentic, bout of pleasure. Real happiness occurs when we intentionally choose to have positive thoughts and emotions—thoughts and emotions that external factors cannot alter. It is in this that happiness must be internalized. While negativity in life is absent of positivity, positivity is not the absence of negativity. Rather, when negativity exists or surfaces, one chooses the application of positive thinking. Positivity, therefore, is intentional truth and light. As one chooses to experience greater positivity in life, most often, one will discover true and authentic happiness.

Let's take a closer look at what influences positive emotions. There are many ways to experience positive emotions. My examples pertain to what I believe is the most authentic way to experience these emotions. Some people buy cars. Some people want to make more money. Some people try to lose weight. Some people go to church. Some people volunteer at food pantries. The point is that all positive emotions matter, but there are different degrees of experiencing these positive emotions. All can impact and influence your degree of happiness, but what you'll find as you bring yourself to a state of conscious awareness is that some experiences or things will have a greater impact than others. And who decides which experience or thing provides greater positive emotions? You do.

That's one of the great things about life. You know yourself better than anyone. If the path to your enlightened experience is clear, then take action (*I say enlightened becomes sometimes we are superficial and believe we can achieve happiness if we do what others do*). Happiness is a personal experience, so the path you take must be personal. Running influences my positive emotions. It makes me feel happy. It makes me feel free. But, while some people might enjoy running, others do not. And if you try to force yourself to enjoy running, will that put you in a positive emotional state or a negative emotional state? Positivity was something that I learned early in life, thanks to experiences like receiving Christmas presents from complete strangers. Learning how to be positive is a skill, one that can be honed and artistically crafted to meet the needs of the individual.

We'll continue to use this pillar as we visit different areas of life and discern how we can become more enlightened and more aware, so that we can self–actualize into a life filled with meaning and love.

Chapter 2:
Change of Perspective

"Hunnel, wake up." I heard a voice say near my bunk.

"Hunnel, are you awake?" I heard once more.

I slowly opened one eye and squinted with the other. You know, that point when someone wants you to wake up and you can only muster the energy to open one eyelid to see what he wants. As I tried to make out the shadowy figure who stood next to my bunk, a bright light hit my face.

"Hunnel," I heard once more. "Wake up now."

As I started to come to, I recognized the voice of the man who stood next to my bunk. Although, I had just met him a few days ago, I knew the hefty and deep intonation in his voice. His flashlight filled all that I could see. I slowly reached for my glasses and put them on. I blinked a couple more times to moisten my eyes and the blurry figure of a face became clearer. His silver hair was combed, but slightly messed up. His age imposed many wrinkles on his face. You could tell that he smiled a lot from the permanent wrinkles at the corners of his eyes and just beyond the corners of his mouth—although now was far from smiling. He

29

wasn't very tall, because he stood the same height as the top of my bunk where I lay. As I looked him in the eyes, I could tell something was off. Something wasn't right. He looked very pale white and his eyes were opened wide and full of concern.

"First Sergeant?" I asked. "What's going on? It's the middle of the night."

"I've got something to tell you," he said, quickly.

I immediately thought to myself, "What could he need from me so early in the morning?"

I quickly turned my attention back to him. "What's going on?" I asked.

"I just received a call from your unit," he replied.

I pondered what on earth would be going on in my unit that would warrant a wakeup just after midnight.

He continued, "A vehicle was struck by an IED and one of the soldiers didn't make it."

My mind began racing. I started going through all the names of the guys I knew. Their faces scrolled through my mind like a vintage movie reel. My heart began to sink as I prepared myself to hear who it was. I took one last swallow before I asked— the type of swallow you make when you are afraid, when your esophagus feels constricted and you notice the tension as your muscles go through their programmed response to push the saliva from your mouth towards your stomach.

I slowly asked, "Who was it?"

My mind was prepped to grieve.

"Castner," my first sergeant hesitantly stated. "Stephen Castner."

I searched my memory to recall if I knew that name. It sounded familiar but I could not picture his face. Suddenly, a rush of emotions hit me like a brick wall. I started to think about what happened to this man. Only three days in Kuwait and we just lost a soldier, a person, a soul. I thanked the first sergeant for telling me the news and then lay back in bed, eyes wide open. I continued to search my memories to see if I knew Stephen. I could not. I wondered what Stephen was like. I wondered why he joined the Army. I wondered what his hobbies were. I wondered about how much pain he experienced before passing.

And as I continued to think about his life and who he was, tears welled up in my eyes. Here I was in a safe building, air conditioning, a bed to lie upon. I was safe. He was not. I felt guilt. I felt shame. He had to endure one of the worst things in life. I didn't know him, yet I couldn't help but feel connected to him. I knew that we were part of a team, part of something bigger than ourselves. We wore the same uniform and the fact that he was now gone made me sad. I'd lost a brother, even though we'd never met. I began to ponder whether he knew today would be his last day, and, if so, would he have done something differently? Would he have told his parents he loved them once more? Would he have learned to play the guitar or picked up a hobby? Would he have bought a house or found someone to love? I wondered what the people back home were going to do once they found out. What pain and sadness they would

31

experience once they heard that Stephen was gone.

At twenty-one years old, this was tough for me to handle. I'd never had anyone that I'd known pass away to this point. And as I pointed out, although I didn't know Stephen, I still felt connected. A few days later I attended his funeral at a military base on the border between Iraq and Kuwait, about an hour and a half from where I was stationed. I drove up there specifically for him that day. It was as hot as hot could be. Sand covered everything. The air was thick. You could feel the heat enter your lungs, almost like being in a sauna.

I made my way to the formation, trudging through the rocks and sand and onto the pavement. Everything seemed to mesh together: the buildings, the land, everything. It was depressing to look at. Our surroundings were either white, black, brown, or a slight variation of those colors. There were no vibrant colors. No green grass or tall trees. No beautiful blue lakes or streams. All seemed dull and lifeless. I stood in formation as the commander took us through the ceremony. Hundreds of us stood there. I could tell many were deep in thought, just as I was. My brain couldn't process the words that were said. All I could focus on was the life of this man, Stephen Castner.

At the conclusion of the ceremony, I walked up to the memorial, which is constructed for each service member who loses his life in battle. At the base were the boots, suede tan, neatly placed with the heels touching together and the toe box pointing outward forming a precise 45-degree angle. Rising from the boots stood the M-4, a semi–automatic rifle. Its black complexity and steel sprouted up with the muzzle faced towards the ground. At the butt of the rifle, the point that one puts into the armpit to provide stability while firing the weapon, rested a helmet covered with a digital camouflage pattern of different tan and brown colors. Just below the helmet hung the dog tags, placed delicately like an ornament dangling on a Christmas tree. Every so often, the wind would push the tags to catch the sun just right and reflect the light off its metallic surface. Next to the memorial was a picture of Stephen.

I finally had a chance to see his face. I recalled passing him often during our training prior to deployment. As the paralegal for the unit, I conducted business at each of the subordinate units. Rounded chin and cheekbones, with a light complexion and skin tone. Glasses rested on the bridge of his nose. Eyes circular and full of life. A smile that curled from ear to ear. I paid him homage and said a prayer for him and his family, hoping that his family could find healing amidst the devastation of this news.

Even as I sit here and write this story, I can't help but shed a tear. It still saddens me to this day. This experience changed how I saw the world and made me realize that life is precious. Our time on this earth should not be squandered, because we never know how long we've got to tell people we love them, to go after our hopes and dreams or to change the world.

After returning home from deployment, I saw the world differently. Our unit lost three soldiers during deployment. Many of my friends changed. I recall asking a good friend how things were going, and his response: "How do you think you'd feel after getting rockets shot at your vehicle and people trying to kill you?" As someone who had an office job, I had a different perspective on how people changed. Many soldiers in my unit went through some really tough experiences. I saw the shift in their personalities as they became accustomed to what war can do to people. Since I did not have those extremely dangerous experiences, I could clearly see that people were different. Seeing my friends change before my eyes actually changed me.

Returning home gave me a different perception—a perception that became my new, destructive reality. I was glad to be home, don't get me wrong, but something just felt off. I felt like people would make big deals out of what I now considered to be petty. A couple weeks after I got home, I was out at a restaurant, and a man in the booth behind me became extremely obnoxious with the waitress regarding his burger. He complained loudly about the way it was cooked. Anger crept in. I turned around and said, "Chill out, there are worse things in life." That was the G-rated level I was able to muster. I really wanted to tell him off using a list of choice, profane words!

There I was, twenty-two years old, having seen all that my friends went through, and this guy was making a huge deal about his burger. Not on my watch. I noticed my attitude dip quite a bit in the months that followed. I felt angry. I felt pain. I felt hurt. But nothing had happened to me. I hadn't been shot at. No one tried to kill me. Yet, my perspective on the experiences of my fellow soldiers changed how I saw things; and life became very unclear. I began to drink—a lot. Alcohol seemed to take away any edge that I felt. The more I had, the better I felt, or so I thought.

I woke up one morning to get ready for class at the local college. I felt angry that morning. It seemed that no matter what I wanted to feel, I couldn't move past the anger. So, I went to the cabinet, poured myself three shots, and stared at them for a few minutes. I stood there, because I knew what it would mean if I drank them. It would confirm what I've already begun to think of myself—that I had an alcohol problem. "Screw it," I thought. "I need this right now!" I drank each shot. As the 90-proof liquor burned down my throat, I could hear something inside me telling me to stop, telling me that I didn't need it, telling me that I was going to be okay. But I didn't listen. I continued. Life became a blur. Life became a struggle. Life became an addiction. My vision was tainted. I was mentally and spiritually blind.

I think sometimes many of us live our lives without a clear vision of who we are and who we want to become. We live day by day, doing the same things over and over. We talk about change, but never really act on it. We make the same choices, complain about the same things, make excuses as to why things will never get better, and we call it life. We value the things others have more than our own. We value the way others live more than how we live. We value others' experiences more than our own. My experiences, struggles, and failures were all necessary for me to transcend into the person I was meant to be. Your experiences, struggles, and failures were all necessary for you to have the opportunity to transcend into the person you were meant to be. It is only through a state of conscious choice that you can clear away of all the garbage and pain to realize what your passions are.

Living with passion can help provide valuable insight into who you are as a person. But it doesn't just stop there. You must live it. Remember your favorite childhood game, activity, or toy. I loved playing checkers. The strategy, the thrill, the suspense. It's a simple game with a simple objective: obtain all the opponent's pieces before your opponent obtains yours. If you could get one of your pieces to the other side by using adjacent, diagonal movement, then you could say, "King me!" I had many passions as a kid. Some I've outgrown. Some I still have, like eating ice cream. My point is, when we were kids and the world was less complicated, we did what was important to us. We had passions in life and we acted upon them. Somewhere along the way, we become extremely serious and self-critical. Now, while some of those qualities may provide a certain purpose, having and living your passion is crucial. It's the underlying force that drives you to pursue things that make you happy.

In the previous chapter, I mentioned how important positive emotional experiences are for the development of the personality, to live happily, and have an exceptional life. Passions create opportunities for you to experience those positive emotions. Living with passion enables you to also live in the present. When you make passion part of life, you don't have to find the motivation to do things, the motivation to do things finds you. The energy finds you. The momentum finds you. Most people don't consciously recognize their passions. If your passions aren't clear to you, then how can you make the choice to pursue them? Your passion generates momentum and fuels your purpose (which we'll talk about during the next chapter). When you get crystal clear on what's important to you, life will unfold into an amazing experience filled with abundance and positivity.

I recently went to the eye doctor to have my vision checked. I could tell that my contacts weren't getting the job done as well as they used to. That meant my vision was getting worse. I showed up at the optometrist's office, ready to get the exam over with. First, I had to fill out all the proper paperwork—name, age, address, insurance carrier, the list goes on and on. Once I completed that, the doctor led me back to a little room with a table. On the table were two little devices: one tonometer, which tests for glaucoma, and the other device which tests visual acuity.

After these two tests, the doctor led me back to the main examination room. It was dark. I sat in a large chair with four different arms branching out from it. At the end of each arm was a large, oval-shaped contraption. To the left of the chair sat a sink, a desk, and chair. On the right was a shelving unit with their respective brands of contacts by type and power neatly organized in specific order. The doctor continued testing. She turned lights off and flipped the switch to a lamp that placed a blurry image (projected eye chart) on the wall.

"Okay, Aaron," she said. "Why don't you cover up your right eye and read to me the smallest line can see clearest."

"Oh great," I thought to myself, "I can't read a single line." My farsightedness had gotten to the point where I couldn't even see the largest letter at the top.

"Umm," I stuttered, "I can't read a single line."

"Okay," she replied, "Let's go with the other eye." I switched hands and covered up my left eye with my left hand. My right eye took a few seconds to adjust to the lighted letters on the wall in front of me. Once again, I couldn't make out any of the letters projected on the wall.

"Nothing," I said. "I still can't see anything."

"Okay," she replied, "Let's get things cleared up for you, shall we?"

The doctor reached out and manipulated two of the different arms affixed to the chair I sat on. She moved them in and put the large oval-shaped contraptions up to my eyes. I placed my chin on the chin rest and pressed my forehead up against the top band for a nice, comfortable resting spot. As she moved the devices in towards my face, she lined up what appeared to be little lenses through which one could peer. As I looked through these lenses, I saw the lighted lettering system up on the wall.

"Okay," she said, "based on your vision history, we're going to start with a baseline lens that should help you see clearer."

"Okay," I said. "Let's do this."

She adjusted the contraptions on each side of my eye, scrolling through the lenses. It sounded like gears turning, click, click, click. Then she stopped. I peered forward and could now see the letters on the wall.

"E," I declared, "I can finally see the largest letter."

"Great!" she stated. "Keep looking at the letters. If this is one—" (she quickly changed the lens) "—and that's two, which is clearer?"

"Two." I answered.

"Okay. How about now... one—" she quickly changed the lens once more "—or two?"

"One." I replied.

She continued this pattern until I could read some of the most difficult lines available. "Wow, that's pretty good," she stated.

"Thanks," I responded. I appreciate all of your help."

It was in this moment that I realized that the process of looking through a series of different lenses helps us see clearly. Just like in life.

We wonder through life with no clear directive or direction. Things seem fuzzy, blurry, a mess. That was how I felt when alcohol ruled my life. I spent every evening drowning my sorrows in at least a six-pack. Negative emotions plagued me, but I barely felt them because of intoxication of my mind, body and spirit. When I drank, I gave myself false happiness because, as I pointed out earlier, true happiness only results from repetitive positive emotions and experiences. I had no positive emotions; I was only numbing the pain. I became desensitized to the world, my emotions, and my life. Alcohol took me to a very dark place. Many people told me I had a problem, which fueled the fire to my self-pity, angst, and pain.

Chapter 3:
Intervention

During my second deployment I picked up running. I didn't like running at first, In fact, I despised it. Were it not for a mere coincidence, running might have never come to be so important in my life.

I remember checking my email on February 16, 2011, almost a year after returning home and taking classes at the local college. I sat in the computer room checking email, miserable since I couldn't stop stressing over a test coming up later that week. Life grew terrible again. I fell back into old patterns of alcohol after about a year of sobriety (because you can't drink while you're deployed). Each morning, I showed up to class anticipating the afternoon's drinking. I'd pass out early enough to get enough sleep to at least be able to function in class the next day. Lather, rinse, repeat.

This email from the Boston Athletic Association played a big role in changing that downward spiral. It read:

SSG Hunnel,

Regrettably, I cannot find that you ever received a response to your email prior to this time,

The Boston Athletic Association has a proud history of working with our active duty military personnel that have been unable to qualify or register for Boston because of a deployment to Iraq or Afghanistan.

Even at this late date, I am able to accommodate your entry to 2011 Boston Marathon if you still have the interest and schedule to be able to register.

Kindly let me know as soon as possible as we are close to finalizing entrants for 2011.

Thank you for your service to our country.

I look forward to hearing from you.

Barbara

Four months prior to this, I emailed the Boston Athletic Association (BAA) asking if they made exceptions for service members who ran the Boston Marathon satellite race in Iraq to qualify for the actual marathon in Boston, MA. For those of you who might not be aware, Boston is a dream race for any marathon runner. Qualifying for this event is extremely difficult. You must be exceptionally fast. I believe the qualifying time for my age group during 2011 was three hours ten minutes, meaning that I would have to run at about seven minutes and fifteen seconds per mile for 26.2 miles. I could barely run one mile at that pace, let alone an entire marathon. I didn't hear back from them, so I figured it was a lost cause... until this email popped into my life.

Without hesitation, I sent my registration form and money to the BAA. As soon as I hit that send button, negative emotions and thoughts flooded my mind: fear, doubt, worry. I had not run at all in almost five months. Whether you've run before or not, it's easy to wrap your mind around the fact that training for only two months before a marathon (especially after your first was a nightmare and you vowed never to do it again) is a very, very bad idea. Not only was I in poor physical shape, I was an emotional and spiritual wreck. Alcohol was ruining everything: my school, my work, my friendships, my marriage, my entire life! However, this opportunity brought a shimmer of hope. In this opportunity, I felt I had a chance to do something worthwhile. As scared as I was, I took the risk—a leap of faith.

Getting into the Boston Marathon was quite the extravaganza. I remember telling my chemistry professor, a running enthusiast, when I received an entry into the Boston Marathon, that I was going to be missing class. It's amazing how life continues to work amidst the struggle and pain.

My professor reached out to the school newspaper to inform them of the race that I would be running in about two months' time. Editorial staff asked if they could meet with me to cover the story. I obliged, and shared my journey with them, albeit leaving out the fact that I was a complete mess at

43

that point in time. They asked if they could recommend the story to the local newspaper. I obliged once more, and was later contacted by the local newspaper within the week. They interviewed me shortly thereafter and took a picture of me running down the street. I wore the Boston Marathon shirt I had received for running in Iraq the year prior. It was electric yellow with three blue pin stripes running (no pun intended) down the length of the long sleeve. In my hand I clasped a blue leash which was attached to the collar of my black lab, Denver. That picture and the story went right on the front cover of the sports section.

When I saw myself, I felt ashamed. I wasn't good enough to be on this cover. I had so many problems in my life then, and there I was, looking happy, out enjoying a nice run with my dog. Running in the Boston Marathon was a runner's dream and I could barely get myself out of bed every morning, mainly from being hungover. And my story was the one that got told?

There were so many other people out there who were worthier, more deserving than I was. I felt inadequate and guilty. The picture made me look happy, energetic, and confident; but, I was far from any of those things. That's when I received a telephone call from the BAA.

"Hi, Aaron, this is Jack, from the BAA," he said.

"Hello," I responded. "What can I do for you?"

"Well, Aaron, your local newspaper contacted us to confirm their story, and we were wondering if you'd like to come up a bit early and be one of our honorees for Patriot's Day?"

I was speechless and confused. Things like this weren't supposed to happen to people like me. I quickly mustered up as many excuses as I could.

"Wow, thanks for asking. But I only have a hotel for one night."

Hotel rooms during the marathon are extremely expensive as they run (no pun again) about $400 to $500 per night. Thank God for a little divine intervention, because my mother-in-law was able to find a friend with whom I could stay and cover half the cost of the room. This was a solid excuse.

"Well, Aaron," he continued, "we'll take care of your room for the first couple of nights."

They wanted me to come on Thursday and the race wasn't until Monday.

"Quick," I thought. I sputtered, I needed another excuse... "Um, thank you, Jack."

I was trying to avoid this great opportunity. I pushed against fate with all my might and it continued to push back.

"My flight comes in on Sunday, so I won't be able to participate. Thanks, though."

I knew this was the nail in the coffin. They had far too many things to worry about. They weren't going to take the time or the money to do this for me. I realize now that I was trying to accommodate my low self–esteem, my low self–worth, and confirm the way I saw and felt about myself.

"Aaron," Jack said, "I don't think you understand what I'm saying."

Clearly, I didn't, because I was trying to find reasons why I shouldn't go.

"We will take care of your flight. We'll take care of your room. We'll take care of your food. All you need to do is show up, do a press conference, say a few words from your marathon experience in Iraq. That's it. We'll take care of the rest. Are you interested?"

Thoughts raced through my mind. I was stuck. I had no excuses left in the tank.

Life was calling me, giving me opportunities to succeed. The harder I pushed and tried to avoid answering that call, the harder life pushed back. It was time. Time to stop feeling sorry for myself. Time to stop thinking about all the bad in my life. Time to stop doing the same thing day after day. My life is going nowhere. This is it. My time has come! Answer that call!

"Okay, Jack. I'll do it."

We ended the conversation thanking each other for the time. I mentally prepared myself as I realized exactly what I had just done. I was about to do a press conference and a speech at an organized event. I quickly got with my English professor to help me prepare a great speech that I could deliver during my time in Boston. We put our heads together and decided that telling the legend of Pheidippides when he ran from Marathon to Athens to declare victory over the Persians. This illustrious story would become the birth to modern-day marathon running, which seemed like a relevant and worthwhile story in my speech.

46

I arrived in Boston just over a month later, ready to experience this once-in-a-lifetime opportunity. Some BAA volunteers greeted me and introduced me to the Hartley family. That's when I met Clarence, the other honoree for Patriot's Day. He stood slightly taller than I, with curly silver hair. He was a slender man with a defined jaw structure and cheekbones. The wrinkles on his face and neck showed his age. His voice was soft and tender.

Clarence had an amazing story. A retired Lieutenant Colonel and pilot in the Air Force, he picked up running in his late sixties because it "looked like fun." Over the next ten years, Clarence was diagnosed with non-Hodgkins Lymphoma and prostate cancer, both of which he beat. Clarence told me that running helped him beat cancer. Even when he was going through treatment, he ran. In his eighties and still passionate about running, he refused to let adverse conditions keep him from doing what he loved.

Clarence inspired me. His strength made me realize that we are capable of doing extraordinary things in our lives. Clarence ran the Boston Marathon in 2011 at the age of eighty-one years old. Although, he has since passed from this world, his story continues to inspire me and others to pursue experiences important to us. Experiences that improve us. Experiences that ignite our passion.

Clarence and I made our way downtown to the Cheer's bar for the Patriot's Day celebration. (Yes, it's the same Cheer's from the famous American TV show that ran from 1982 to 1993.) The time had come for me to deliver my speech. The room was crowded and dark, except for the podium where I would later stand to address the group. Fear consumed me. Like most people, I hated public speaking. I did not want to go up to that podium and talk. I'd rather do anything else. But it didn't matter. I had committed myself to this, and I would follow through. I embraced the ounce of courage I could muster up, a sheer difference from the negativity, turmoil and pain I'd experienced over the past several weeks.

A tall man walked up to the podium. The crowd grew silent to listen to him. He was the man who would introduce me. I quickly quieted my thoughts so I could listen attentively and wait for his cue.

The first sentence out of his mouth went something like this: "Have you heard about the story of Pheidippides?"

"Oh, crap!" I thought. "That was the story I had worked hard on for my speech! That's my story! What am I going to do now?"

I had only minutes before he would call me to the podium. My anxiety rose, my heart rate increased. I felt like I was going to implode.

"We have a service member who ran our satellite race last year in Iraq," I heard him say.

"Shoot. I'm literally going up there right now. What am I going to do?"

I smiled as I walked towards the podium, not knowing what to say and wishing to be anywhere in the world but here. Despite all the uncertainty and fear, I looked at the crowd and decided I should just speak from the heart. That's when it happened. I discovered that I was stronger than I had given myself credit. I was more valuable than I had previously believed. It was now time for me to unlock the doors that would lead me to my own personal greatness.

I said: "Sometimes, things in life happen that stress you out. For example, I was about to tell the story of Pheidippides during my speech, but, thanks to Tim, I no longer have to do that."

I got a good chuckle out of the crowd.

"So, when life throws a curve ball and tries to stress you out and bring you down, what do you do? You run, but you don't run away from it, you run through it."

I became confused as to why everything clicked so naturally. It defied everything I had just experienced moments ago, with all the shame, fear, and doubt. I felt this entrenched sense of energy as I spoke. I didn't write any of this, neither did I rehearse it; I just spoke from my heart and it felt amazing!

"Being deployed is stressful. You're away from your friends, your family, and everything you know to be true. Everything you know to be safe. Everything you know to be comfortable. Finding things you are passionate about can make all the difference in being able to overcome stress, uncertainty, and fear. I ran the marathon in Iraq because I wanted a t-shirt and medal. But what I found in running was a passion. It gave me something to work towards and challenge myself. Even though it made me feel accomplished, I vowed never to do it again—that is until you called.

And now here I am if front of you ready to conquer this race one more time."

Was this me talking? Running? A passion? It made me feel better. Every word I spoke lifted a burden from my life. I was releasing all the negative talk and unworthiness I had spent so much time thinking and saying. I finished my speech by thanking everyone for their support and willingness to listen to my story. The audience applauded and I stepped down wondering what the heck I just did. I felt awesome, invigorated, and energized!

Chapter 4:

Passion

I ran the Boston Marathon a couple of days later. That experience provided great insights into my life. One, I realized that running was something that, deep down, I was passionate about. And two, I felt extremely energized after overcoming my fear of speaking by moving beyond self-doubt and tapping into what my heart was telling me. I took that courage and metaphorically put it in my pocket as I traveled back home.

Sometimes, we live not knowing what we are passionate about and fail to seek opportunities that help us discover our passions. Check your life right now and ask yourself, "Do I incorporate activities or experiences in my life that I'm passionate about?" As you ponder this question, let's take a look at the science of passion.

Total well-being isn't the absence of disease, but rather the total presence and harmonizing of your mind, body, and spiritual experiences. Living with passion is not limited to happiness; it also includes self-growth and life satisfaction. A positive emotional state yields many physical health benefits which contribute to the human experience. Doing activities that you are passionate about creates a sense of harmony in your life. You will feel energized to do the things that are important to you.

Robert Vellerand, a social psychologist and researcher at the University of Montreal in Quebec, provides valuable insight into the role that passion plays in our lives. He states that passion can improve our health, relationships, and performance. Specifically, he evaluates how passion contributes to greater psychological well-being and how it affects our daily lives. In an article titled, "The role of passion in sustainable psychological well–being," he writes that the concept of passion began as a philosophical query that examined aspects of passion as both a degree of motivation and a degree of suffering (e.g., the crucifixion of Jesus is said to be "passion" because of the suffering he endured). In short, we become "slaves" to our passion.

Vellerand argues on behalf of René Descartes, a seventeenth century French philosopher, that passions bring about strong emotional tendencies which influence behavior. What matters most is the "reason that underlies that behavior." Such a reason can compel us to act and experience our most abundant potential. He goes on to point out, specifically, that passion can serve a dual role in our lives. We must consciously be aware of whether its implications serve as something that facilitates harmony or obsession. Harmonious passion occurs when we autonomously associate an activity with something that is pleasurable and that we can see ourselves continuing to engage in more frequently. We can like and, in some cases, love a given activity. It can become part of us and interweave the energy derived from partaking in the activity into the fabric of our personality. It influences us, moves us, and gives us light.

In my case, running is a passion of mine. I do it frequently because I thoroughly love it. I don't just engage in the activity; I consider myself a "runner." Similarly, someone who is passionate about flying planes isn't merely a person who merely engages in flying planes. No, that person is a pilot. Someone who is passionate about drawing pictures and creating art doesn't merely engage in the activity of drawing or creating art; he or she is an artist.

There is a tipping point to this, as Vellerun points out. Sometimes our passions can lead to obsessive patterns wherein the internalization of these activities results in becoming more rigid because of the "lack of flexibility via intra- or extra-personal influences for self-esteem or social status." You've probably seen or experienced this first-hand at some point in your life. For example, a child finds something that interests him or her and engages in the activity. Maybe it's swimming, playing the piano, or learning. As time goes on, the child develops a unique bond with the activity. Consequently, it becomes a passion. As the love for the activity increases, the frequency of performing the activity increases. Some parents begin to recognize the potential: the child does well because he or she enjoys or even loves the activity. Parents may continue to push via an extra-personal relationship, thereby engulfing the child in the activity. The child does it every day, for hours a day, even on weekends, not by choice, but by command. The child's schedule becomes rigid with little room for flexibility to choose or even experience the activity in a way that made him or her fall in love with it in the first place. It becomes an obsession.

Another example of obsessive passion could be the desire to accumulate financial wealth due to the social pressure to conform. I am an advocate for accumulating wealth, because I believe that wealth can create more value and more opportunities for people in the world. If I were to want a certain car, for example, merely because I believed it would confer a certain social status, then arguably the intra- and extra-personal relationship (external pressure from friends or colleagues, and internal pressure from myself to conform) could drive me (no pun) to an extremely inflexible and intolerable life. I'd argue a bit further that this is not passion at all, but more plainly an extrinsic source of motivation (which we'll discuss a bit later).

Passion is an enlightened form of living, because it invokes some of our deepest desires. When we are in tune with our deepest desires, the unfolding of our lives can become quite remarkable. Continue to develop a strong relationship with activities or things that you are passionate about. Don't go after social status, go after what's important to you and what makes you feel excited, energized, vibrant, or even zesty!

Here are some questions that you may ask to discover or reconnect with a passion in life:

- What are my values and beliefs, and how can I

align those with an activity?

- What will make me feel good about myself?

- What talents do I have that could be put to good use?

- What makes me feel energized just by thinking about it?

- Will this make me feel like I am living life on my own terms?

- What new insights can I continue to uncover as I pursue this activity?

As you answer and explore these questions, allow your conscious thinking to take over. Lead with your heart and search what you feel. Your logical brain, the one which helps you analyze and process certain pieces of information so that you can categorize and rationalize your degree of adequacy, may try to assume command. It will tell you that you don't have experience or that you are not good enough to even try a certain activity. In the logical brain, you will find fear and doubt, because those rationalization techniques help us determine what is safe and what is not. While that type of thinking may prove useful in some situations, it is not always helpful. It inhibits our ability to reach beyond what we believe we are capable of achieving and often results in a phenomenon called "analysis paralysis." This type of thinking feeds mediocrity and limits all the potential living within you. Consciously look past the logic and get right into the emotion. Committing to the positive experience prior to the rationalization—or irrationalization, because, quite honestly, that's what it is—expands your horizons, enhances fluidity, and creates the space in your personality and your life to pursue that which is important to you. Thus, you will contribute to your positive emotional state, a state in which happiness can grow.

I have many passions. Running is a passion that I have maintained for numerous years. Since I gave that speech at the Cheer's lounge in Boston, I have developed other passions, too. The next chapter connects the dots on what it means to live with positivity, passion, and—last but not least—purpose.

Chapter 5:
Purpose

The anecdotes up to this point set the stage for what I believe to be the greatest acquisition in my life: purpose. Purpose is much more than a mere reason for doing something that you want to do, or something that you enjoy—which is passion. It's much deeper than that. Passion gives light to the personality. Purpose gives light to the soul. It embodies the very reason of your existence. It defines all that you are and were meant to fulfill on this planet and in this life. As I continue with some excerpts from my life, pay keen attention to the relationship that underlies your positivity, passion, and purpose. You will notice that each of these pillars is not mutually exclusive, meaning that they don't act independently of one another. Rather, they act in relationship with one another. No one is more important than the other, for all pillars influence each other. All are interconnected. It only adds to the complexity of life and the unique algorithms constantly at work which inhibit or enhance our chances for happiness, health, and success.

My heart felt heavy as I knelt during a prayer at the conclusion of church. I reflected on the previous day I spent with a friend from Iraq. As veterans, we were invited to attend a college football game at the University of Wisconsin. As part of the experience, we went onto the field before the game and held the American flag during the National Anthem. It was a hot day in August and life seemed to be improving for me in the four months after running in the Boston Marathon, meeting Clarence, and connecting with an amazing running community. In the months after running a second marathon, I found a joy, a passion for running, and even more so, for endurance events. As such, I had made up my mind that I wanted to try an IRONMAN triathlon.

The pinnacle endurance race for any endurance athlete, the IRONMAN consists of a 2.4-mile swim, a 112-mile bicycle ride, and a 26.2-mile run. I spent a lot of mental energy mustering up the courage and the belief that I could, at some point, complete a distance of that magnitude. In preparation, I quit drinking and using tobacco (another addiction that plagued my life for about eight years) about two weeks prior to that hot, blistery, summer day in August at Camp Randall, the stadium where the Wisconsin Badgers play. Motivated to stick to my guns about not drinking and using tobacco, I avoided alcohol during the tailgating portion of the game.

After the National Anthem, we went back to our site to grab a few things. Some friends asked if I wanted a beer. Everything inside me screamed, "No, Aaron, don't do it!" I had gone weeks without drinking or using tobacco—the longest time I'd managed to avoid both in quite a while. I was ready for a new me, a new chance at life, a shot at doing an IRONMAN but I felt pressure to conform. All the resistance I could muster wasn't enough. I gave in. As I drank that ice cold beer, I immediately felt shame and regret. I told myself to stop, but I could not. All I wanted to do was to stop those negative emotions and feelings from flooding my mind. If I had quit, then I would have found the courage and hope in that experience. However, my logical brain convinced me—because I knew how easy it was to numb the pain with alcohol—that continuing to drink would be the best choice. So, that's what I did. I drank until I couldn't feel the pain anymore. As much as I didn't want to, I chose to harm my body, my mind, and my spirit, even though I knew it would come at a great cost. As a result of my inhibited judgment, I asked for some chewing tobacco from my friend on the ride home. By that point, my shame had returned and I felt like a complete failure.

That day, that experience, was the lowest point in my entire life. I had officially hit rock bottom. If you've ever hit rock bottom, then you can likely recall that we are literally presented with two options. First, stay where you are—a very unhealthy and ugly life to live. Or, second, look up, get up, and move Upwards. I chose the latter, or should I say the latter chose me.

I reflected on that pitiful day while I knelt in that pew. I felt nauseated, tired and stressed. My mouth was dry and body hurt. Maybe you believe in God, or maybe you don't. I questioned the existence of God quite often growing up. Living in the house of a pastor gave me insight into the anger and hypocrisy of people who called themselves Christians. Also, if God was so good, then why were these people ruining others' lives? Why were they talking about love and forgiveness, yet instigating pain and suffering into their own lives, their families' lives, and the lives of their communities? I saw the rawness, the evil, of the human spirit and its drive for self-pleasing decision-making, all at the cost of love, hope, and joy.

But I was desperate as I sat in church. I did something that I didn't normally do: I consciously prayed. At that moment, I felt a sensation unlike anything I had ever felt. Its warmth lifted all the emotional baggage I carried. I felt safe. I felt strong. I marveled at that experience, enjoying what I believe to be the most transcendent of all human experiences: grace. You can challenge the existence of God; but there is something transformational once you accept the notion that He does actually exist.

This is not merely a point to argue the existence of God; but, rather, testimony that I found God at the moment when I was meant to find Him. There is something in the human spirit that connects us all. If you have not sought your own spiritual enlightenment, then how can you say God doesn't exist? That was the exact question I asked myself.

I let go of any and all resistance during that moment of grace and felt something I had not felt in a very long time—joy, happiness, love, peace. It was the same overwhelmingly positive concoction of emotions that flooded me during that Christmas years ago.

I now realize that I wasn't experiencing just the compassion of the human spirit; I was experiencing God. I no longer questioned His existence because my spirit now felt complete.

I made choices within the past twelve hours that kept me from living, learning and loving. That moment, I felt like my past no longer defined me, but rather refined me. I had a sense of clarity and energy that I could not explain, except to feel as though everything was about to change—big time! I left church that day with my wife and explained to her that something was different, that something had changed inside me. She agreed that something did seem different.

I now had the ammunition to fire off that which propels us all, energizes us all, and transcends us all: purpose.

Purpose is the derivative of all that you are, and all that you are to become. It's the vision you have for yourself. It's like looking through binoculars and being able to see, with extreme clarity, all that is around you, all that embodies you, and all that defines you. You can see what's ahead in the distance and carry out all that is necessary to move you closer towards your destination. Purpose is fluid. It takes the form of one's experiences and environment that shapes it. It's like water in a bottle. The water takes on the shape of the bottle, yet if you move it to a different container, it will take on that new shape. In this way, water—just like you¬— can adapt and overcome ever-changing environments. Your purpose is yours and yours alone. And as you continue to change in life, your purpose is always there.

61

Many of us, however, fail to actively pursue our purpose. Mostly because of our lack of personal awareness and consciousness, we do not have the insight into our own lives to make such a choice. I do not categorize this lack of consciousness as good or bad. People are exquisite beings with unlimited potential and creative uniqueness. Each experience serves a purpose in an individual's life that is meant to teach something, uncover something, and transform something. Good and bad are categorical words meant to compartmentalize an experience. Furthermore, if something is said to be bad, then it is processed differently in the brain as a negative experience and likely trigger a fear response. Our brain tells us: "This experience is bad. Be afraid of it." I argue that if we are afraid of an experience and see it as bad, then we lose the opportunity to consider the possibility that the experience was not actually bad, but rather necessary. Your perspective shapes what you learn from your experiences. I used to see drinking to excess as bad; but, as I reflect on my past, I now see that alcoholism and addiction were necessary for me to learn and grow as a person. I appreciate all that I have learned from that experience.

Everything in life exists as a relationship. Think of electricity. Because we found a way to create light using electricity, candles no longer serve as our main source of light. Our relationships with candles have diminished while our relationships with electricity-fueled light has strengthened. Now, consider how we've been able to use electricity. It has allowed us to increase connections with friends and family anywhere (I was able to stay connected to my wife during deployments, a privilege that I know not every service member prior to this technology was able to experience—they had to rely on letters). Consider other relationships that increase or decrease over time, and how they affect you, your community or even the world. The increase in fast food restaurants in relationship with our desire for instant gratification contributed to the overconsumption of calories (which again, I see neither good nor bad, but rather what is). Increased prevalence of smart devices and social media apps and games has decreased how much we read newspapers. Increasing science has decreased our faith in certain things. Increasing our technology in powered flight allows us to travel all over the world and even into outerspace (which Virgin is now offering flights for people at $200k a seat).

Something interesting I found out when I returned home from my second deployment was that increasing my relationship with running put me at a greater risk of being attacked by red wing blackbirds. Since I'd never been attacked by a bird of any kind, that was quite a shock.

These birds live on some trails I run on next to the river. Each summer when they have their babies, they line these trails. In some instances, I've seen as many as fifteen in a 300-yard span (only eight of them attacked me). Because I spend time (quantitative time) running during the summer on a particular trail next to the water with a beautiful view, I make myself susceptible to these attacks.

Shooing off these birds as they swoop at my head, I've probably provided a bit of entertainment to drivers passing by.

You've probably heard the phrase from the media before, "If it bleeds, it leads." They understand that, if they cover stories involving rare cases that are scary, or influence a negative emotion, then you're going to watch it. The more we continue to develop these relationships, much like the neural connections in our brains, the stronger the relationships become in our culture and in our society.

I don't identify these as causal relationships, directly causing the other. Rather, these relationships, which are all around us, drive other behaviors, attitudes, beliefs, and results. Your mind, in essence, is comprised of a collection of relationships, some stronger than others, and some more influential than others. Your life is also made up of a collection of relationships. Some stronger than others, and some more influential than others. Which relationships limit you and which ones lift you—*Upwards*.

Let's take a look at some other examples we might categorize as "bad." As a health and wellness professional, I hear many people call a cookie, an icecream bar, or a glass of Gatorade "bad." I don't eat an entire box of cookies or icecream bars in one sitting. I don't drink a gallon of Gatorade (which, mind you, fuels my runs) in one day. But I do consume these foods because I enjoy and have developed a healthy relationship with them. Many foods are labeled 'bad' because the individual has developed an unhealthy relationship with that

64

food, albeit from social norms and fear mongering by perceived nutrition experts. You don't label broccoli as "bad." Why not? Well, because most people aren't tempted to eat broccoli to excess. It's not the food or the temptation which is "bad," but rather your relationship with that food or temptation.

It's a deeper understanding. It's in your perspective. This is a subsequent factor of your purpose. Food becomes part of you, part of your cells, which enables your body to live, to move, to think, to breathe, and to be. That's how I see food.

Now, if I were in the middle of a desert, starving, and still days away from civilization and if my only choices were cookies, ice cream bars, and Gatorade, which would be "bad" for me? I would eat all of them, because they would provide the fuel I need to keep me alive. Food, a lifestyle metaphor of daily experiences such as doing something you are passionate about, and opening your mind to emotions such as positivity, serve you as part of a bigger purpose. The "bad" you see is present when you look through the lens of fear, and the "good" you see is present when you look through the lens of love.

Fear deteriorates relationships, while love builds relationships. If you only see situations or experiences as good or bad, as absolute, rather than intentionally increasing awareness about the lens through which you are looking, then you miss out on greater understanding and insight, trumped by logic and other irrational, cognitive processes. Your purpose governs all that you see, all that you think, and all that you do. All that you choose to see, think, or do governs your purpose. It all exists as a relationship, neither good nor bad, but constantly informing you of whether all that you are, and all that you are becoming, is in alignment with your purpose.

It took me a while to find and understand the role that a conscious, living, breathing purpose can have in life. Serving in the military definitely gave me a sense of meaning and purpose. It made (and still makes) me feel like part of a team and engaged in cause greater than myself. Deployments were stressful, but I learned a great deal from my leaders, friends, and experiences while serving both tours. I had a purpose when I donned that uniform.

There were also times when I was living it, even though it might not have been clear to me. There were times when I had no purpose. I lost that purpose when I came home. My alcoholism and negative mindset resulted from living with no purpose. I saw my life as "bad," because I viewed it through the lens of fear, rather than love. I loved serving as part of a greater cause. Returning to the United States subconsciously took that away from me. I was blindsided by my own ambiguity for determining how to replace that loss. I replaced it with alcohol. Once I realized how important purpose is in life, I intentionally chose to see those experiences as necessary for me to transcend into a more meaningful and purpose-driven life—a life of love.

The many things I learned, that I can now reflect upon, resulted in what I believe to be the most authentic and greatest version of myself. I learned my purpose was to serve others and spread the joy of health and wellness. Ever since that day in church when I experienced surmounting joy, love, and hope, I have no longer felt the need to drink or use tobacco. So, I quit. Just like that, cold turkey. The thing about purpose is that when it's precisely clear, and when you fully commit to it, life doesn't get harder. On the contrary, it gets easier.

Past attempts to give up tobacco and alcohol were difficult because I made them difficult. I had no vision, direction, or purpose for my life. Now that I had those things—vision, direction, and purpose— I had no reason to put things into my life that held me back. My lifestyle changed completely as a result. I added more and more positivity into my life, because it made me feel alive. I began to do what I was passionate about because I knew that life was short. My purpose propelled me to seek that which I found important and valuable. Those experiences, in turn, fueled my purpose and my soul. I became driven and focused.

I started the second half of my education, working towards a degree in health promotion and wellness, a path that now, more than ever, aligned with all that I was and all that I wanted to be. I ran. I learned. I became consciously alive!

Chapter 6:
Turning Point

You can't always make plans for positivity, passion, purpose, or even success to manifest in life. Sometimes, they happen on their own. This chapter describes a critical point in time in my life that put me on an exponential trajectory towards health and happiness.

It was just another day as I walked into a local running store. I had recently entered a drawing for a GPS run watch and was checking in to see if they had given it away yet. It was a nice, breezy, and cool September day. The last month and a half of no drinking or using tobacco created a unique sense of vividness and vitality. I continued to push on towards my goal to complete an IRONMAN. I felt that if I were to be competitive, I'd first need a bit of technology that helped me determine how fast I was going. I walked up to the counter to inquire about the GPS.

"Sorry," the clerk stated. "We just gave it away and unfortunately you didn't win."

A little let down, I brushed it off and started looking around the store to see if there was anything that I needed for my runs. As I made my way over to the shoes, my wife, who had accompanied me to the store called for me.

"Hey, Aaron, come over here," She said. "There's someone I want you to meet."

I turned my attention towards them and made my way over. Next to my wife stood a young couple. A blonde woman with hair down to her shoulders, a light complexion, and a smile on her face. She stood next to who I assumed to be her husband. He stood taller than most men, maybe six feet and one or two inches. Standing up straight, you could see his slender build. He had shorter hair, and like his wife, light skin tone.

"Hello," I said as I made my way up to them. I extended my hand out to the woman first, since it seemed that my wife knew her best.

"Hi," She replied with enthusiasm. "I'm Laura. Marissa and I went to high school together. That's how we know each other."

I quickly glanced over at Marissa and gave her a quick smile.

"Wow," I said, "that's really cool."

"And this is my husband Brian," she continued. "He's a big runner."

I extended my hand out and shook his hand.

"Hello, I'm Aaron," I replied. "Nice to meet you. So you are a runner, what kind of distances do you do?"

I figured maybe he did marathons at best. I mean I'd never really heard of anyone going a distance longer than that.

"Well," he said, "I'm doing some charity work right now, so I'll be running from Kenosha to Appleton next year. That's what I'm training for."

You probably don't know how far the distance is between these two cities. Neither did I at the time.

"You're running what? How far is that?" I blurted in awe. That had to be over one hundred miles.

"It's about one hundred thirty five miles total," he replied humbly. He was very soft spoken, but you could tell that he was strong.

"That's amazing!" I said. "Why on earth are you running that far?"

"Well," he replied, "I'm running to increase awareness about disabled veterans and the service they provide to our country. It's part of an organization that I'm involved with called my TEAM TRIUMPH. We push athletes with disabilities in specialized running chairs."

In my mind, I thought, "This guy is nuts to run this far, but his purpose for running is admirable." Considering my past experiences with the military, I commended him for his courageous intent.

"I'm having trouble, though," he said openly and honestly. "I have the meaning behind why I want to run this far, but I don't really have any veterans or anyone else that I know who can help me get the message out to these military-affiliated organizations."

Something deep down made me feel that this encounter was not a mere coincidence, but something that was necessary for me to fulfill my purpose.

"Well, I'm a veteran and would be willing to help if I can. I have some connections and can maybe connect you with some people, if you like."

This friendship would become pivotal in my life. We continued our discussion that day, talking passionately about the journey he was about to embark upon and how I could provide some resources to really bring the veteran message to the forefront. We exchanged numbers.

Just before I left, I said, "Wow, crazy we were able to meet up today. If our wives didn't know each other we might never have made this connection."

He smiled and agreed.

"What brought you in today?" I asked. Knowing that a matter of minutes could have made the difference as to whether our wives would see each other or not.

"Well, I entered this drawing for a GPS. They told me I won, so I'm here to pick it up."

My jaw dropped.

"That's funny," I said. I didn't think it was funny. I thought it was amazing, but I was so filled with awe, that's all I could say. "I came in to see if they had drawn a winner for the GPS. I obviously didn't get it."

I was amazed in that moment in awe and shock. So many instances had to fall into place for us to meet each other. Had our wives not attended high school together, we wouldn't have met. Had I not picked up running and given up drinking at the time I did, we wouldn't have met. If I hadn't want to keep pushing and upgrading the equipment I had, we wouldn't have met. If he hadn't won, we wouldn't have met. The list goes on and on. The point of the matter is that there are some experiences, such as these, which you cannot plan for.

Spending time with Brian and getting introduced to myTEAM TRIUMPH would soon prove to have a profound influence on my life. As I reflect on this story, I've come to realize that an opportunity presented itself. I did not plan for it. I did not strategically try to make it happen. This opportunity deeply aligned with my purpose to serve others and spread the joy of health and wellness. Because of this alignment, I felt it was something that I must do.

These types of opportunities manifest in our lives more frequently than you probably imagine. It is only through our unconsciousness that we fail to see and take advantage of these opportunities. Maybe you can remember a time when you took advantage of an opportunity in your life. Or, looking back, a time when you passed on a great opportunity. No matter the case, knowing and living your purpose help you discern when great opportunities present themselves and see the world in a different light.

Organizations, like some people, typically have a purpose. Most are governed by what they call a vision statement. An organization's vision statement describes all that it aspires to be. Take Zappos, for example. Zappos is an online shoe retailer started, in 1999, by Nick Swinmurn. Nick started this business because he recognized the limited choices in traditional shoe warehouses. One could find the right shoe, but not the right color. One could find the right shoe color, but not the right size. He determined that endless shopping hours trying to find the brand of shoe one wanted, in the model one wanted, in the color one wanted, in the size one wanted, was extremely inefficient and stressful. By selling a variety of makes, models, colors, and sizes, they could become a hub for selling the exact shoe a customer wanted—and the best part, the customer could find it in a matter of minutes. Here's Zappos' vision statement:

"One day, 30% of all retail transactions in the US will be online. People will buy from the company with the best service and the best selection. Zappos.com will be that online store.

We believe that the speed at which a customer receives an online purchase plays a very important role in how that customer thinks about shopping online again in the future, so at Zappos.com, we have put a lot of focus on making sure the items get delivered to our customers as quickly as possible. In order to do that, we warehouse everything that we sell, and unlike most other online retailers, we don't make an item available for sale unless it is physically present in our warehouse."

Can you see and feel the clarity that Zappos uses for their vision statement? They articulate with precision exactly who they are and who they want to be. That sense of clarity is necessary to pursue and transcend their fullest potential. I use

Zappos.com as an example, because their purpose informs that type of culture and climate they create for their employees. In Zappos' case, they incorporate the first two pillars, positivity, and passion.

For Zappos, much like any other organization, leadership is key. Tony Hsieh, President and CEO at Zappos, is on the front line with his employees working to ensure that they create and maintain a culture and climate which fosters enthusiasm, well-being, and autonomy. Because the purpose is clear, everything that the organization does ties back into it. They are committed to their purpose in all that they do. New employees at Zappos receive a number of great benefits. One of the greatest benefits is the culture and climate the organization has created around happiness. They use research-based information regarding happiness and strategically devise and innovate opportunities to attract and retain the right talent. They use the phrase "Delivering Happiness" as part of their mantra, which again ties back into their purpose. They believe that if their employees are happy and well taken care of, then they will be better stewards of the brand and better customer service representatives for customers.

Hsieh states in his book, Delivering Happiness, that: "Happiness is really just about four things: perceived control, perceived progress, connectedness (number and depth of your relationships), and vision/meaning (being part of something bigger than yourself)." Culture is the number one priority Hsieh and the rest of the organization focus on, because they believe it will have the greatest impact.

Zappos manifests two very important ideas that support their purpose. First, their organizational structure is not a modern hierarchy like many organizations we see. Zappos avoids the top-down approach in their organization and operates in more of a self–directed, self–governing environment known as Holacracy®. In a Holacracy® employees can challenge predict-and-control paradigms by redistributing the power to the employees to achieve control, which is the first concept Hsieh mentions in the above quotation. Zappos further points out that the purpose of the Holacracy® is for the organization to operate more like a community and less like a bureaucratic corporation. This happens because, as communities grow, innovation and productivity increase. However, as organizations grow, innovation and productivity decrease.

Jim Collins states in his book, Good to Great, that for organizations to be successful, they need to put the right people on the bus. Zappos does exactly that. They will pay a new hire $3,000 to leave the organization within the first week. I really like this strategy for two reasons. First, it will get the right type of people on the bus. You can filter out employees who won't be a good fit, should they happen to get hired, if they make it about the money—which, as Zappos has pointed out, is not their first priority. Second, it shows a great deal of trust. The organization bets that their culture, their climate, and their operations are so exceptional that you'll stay. And it shows. Only three percent of new employees take the deal.

Using these innovations and methodologies to emphasize a positive and happy culture ties into everything that they do—their purpose. As a result of doing exactly what they set out to do, they make money. In 2015, they earned over $2 billion in revenue all while having only 1500 employees.

Writing your purpose isn't something you can do superficially. It must become part of you, much like Zappos' vision/purpose is ingrained in all that they do.

You don't have to wait to discern your purpose. Take a moment and pause right now. Ask yourself, "What's my purpose?" As you think to yourself, create a vision in your mind of your ideal or greatest self. What do you see yourself, doing, being, becoming? What sounds do you hear? What sights do you see? What fragrances do you smell? Developing a purpose requires careful and clear thinking. If you are anxious and stressed as you perform this exercise, add a few deep breaths so you can tap into your present consciousness and clarity. Great. Now maybe you were able to come up with your purpose right away, or maybe you weren't. There is no right or wrong way to do this. Because the purpose lies within you, you are the only one who can find it. If you weren't able to find it yet, then that's okay. It requires a bit of effort and thought to develop your own personal purpose statement. It's not automatic. It's not necessarily fast or immediate. Discern and meditate on your purpose, as it will determine who you become.

For transparency, my purpose changes as I continue to change and evolve. It looks something like this:

My purpose is to change the world by inspiring people to live with positivity, passion, and purpose. I'll serve others as part of my commitment to humanity by spreading the joy of health and wellness. I'll be a father and husband who loves, trusts, and leads by setting an example. I will live, breathe, and be all that I am and all that I aspire to become.

Purpose gives our life light and meaning. It is equivalent to the same energy as the sun. When we know and live our purpose, it is like the sun at noon and its highest in the sky, shining brightly for everything and everyone. When the sun is at its highest point, darkness cannot prevail. At all points throughout the day, while the sun is out, you can see your shadow behind, beside, or in front of you. This is the absence of light. But when the sun is at its highest point, the light reaches almost all places. It surrounds and encompasses everything. The only absence of light is beneath you. The only darkness is under you. That's what purpose does when it is embodied in all that you think, speak, and do. It drives out darkness, because darkness cannot exist where there is light. When you discover your light—your purpose—it will drive out all the inefficiencies, all the unnecessary hypercriticisms, and all the anger and fear, and replace it with love, hope, and happiness.

The Midlife in the United States study (known as MIDUS) reports that those who responded to knowing their purpose in life were more likely to outlive their peers. Gallup also reports that those who have purpose and are not "wondering through life aimlessly," live longer lives. This means that purpose plays a fundamental role in our life and prosperity. It affects us in not just the physical sense, but also in a deep psychological and spiritual sense, all of which are connected. Vic Strecher mentions in his book, Life on Purpose, a study in which over 1500 adults with heart disease were followed for two years. Researchers found that those who had increased purpose on their life scale had a 27 percent reduced risk of suffering from a heart attack. A second study of over 6,000 adults followed over four years found that increased purpose resulted in a 22 percent reduced risk of stroke.

I'm not saying that there is a direct causation between having a purpose and living a healthier, longer life, nor am I trying to scare you into having a purpose. There are plenty of scare tactics in the media and society, most of which say, "Change or die." That is not my approach. I simply explain these ideas, so that you can become enlightened, and, should you choose, seek opportunity in and around purpose. Positive emotions, strong social relationships, and even your life's purpose are all keys that unlock doors to greater well-being.

Knowing and living your purpose in life can enhance the quality of your relationships, provide you with greater positive emotions that influence good health, and, ultimately, empower you to live up to your potential. How many Americans know their purpose? Gallup reports that about 37 percent of Americans are thriving in purpose, like what they do each day and are motivated to achieve their goals. This leaves 63 percent of us suffering and struggling to find and live a meaningful life. So, what can we do to find direction, meaning, or happiness in life?

Knowing your purpose can increase the clarity of meaning for your life. Maybe it's to be the best parent you can be. Maybe it's helping people and volunteering at charitable organizations. Maybe it's leading people or building successful teams. Whatever your purpose is, it will help clarify what you want in life. The greater the clarity, the better you'll be committed to your goals, dreams, and aspirations. One thing that comes to mind in these studies is that having a purpose and living a purpose are two completely separate ideas. Having a purpose is knowing what your purpose is. You can have a purpose, one which you know very well, and not take the necessary action to align your life with your purpose. Those who benefit from purpose are the ones who take action to live it. Living your purpose must be a meaningful and conscious choice—one made every single day. The more you focus on and live your purpose, the clearer your purpose becomes. And the clearer your purpose becomes, the more energy light and momentum you receive.

This concludes the framework in which I live my life: positivity, passion, and purpose. Now, that we are consciously aware of the benefits these pillars bring to our well-being, let's examine how daily practice with these ideas can create more and more momentum, opportunity, and success for all that you want in and out of life. Hang tight, we're going for a ride.

What does it mean to synthesize and how can we use this terminology to incorporate more abundance in our lives? Life is hard, right? People are stressed, don't have enough time, and live on autopilot mode through so much of life. We make choices that don't align with our purpose or our passions—choices that decrease our positive experiences in life. Some of us want to change, but we feel like we are stuck in this ambiguous physical, emotional, and spiritual state. We don't feel good, and therefore, we don't make good choices. Now here's the direction that most people take to feel better about themselves, which, for the purpose of this example, is happiness. People want to be happy, so they think that if they work really hard towards something, then they'll find it. I see this all too often in the weight-loss industry. People try to lose weight on diet and supplement programs, because they want to achieve that perceived ideal body type, a "beach body" with beauty and attractiveness. Then, as a result of that accomplishment, they'll feel better about themselves, and ultimately, happier.

The weight-loss industry is a $55 billion industry. Why is that? Most of it hinges on the idea that weight-loss programs don't work for the majority of people. For the people who do find success in those programs, it's a result of discovering positivity and living with passion and purpose. But here's the catch: weight loss is only a means to an end. In most cases, when I ask people what they want from their weight reduction, they simply say, "Happiness." But happiness, as I've pointed out, is so much more complex than losing a few pounds. It's a lifestyle that goes beyond exercising and eating right and transcends into a life of positivity, passion, and purpose. You can't simply remove something and expect everything to change. Losing weight won't make you seek opportunities that create a positive emotional state, do things that you're passionate about or help you discover and live your purpose.

The three P's (Positivity, Passion and Purpose) must be applied. Only then, once you feel happy by applying the three P's, will you make choices, such as exercising and eating healthfully. As a result, you might lose weight, but, then again, you might not. And that's okay, because we're all built differently. For me to transcend into what I believe is my greatest life, I didn't need to remove alcohol, tobacco, and negativity. No, I tried that many times. It didn't work. What I needed to do was apply the three P's and flood my life with them. As a result, all the things that held me back were no longer necessary, because I now discerned my life's path. Everything became so clear and I became so energized, focused, and committed to myself—which I believe to be self-love—all the physical, emotional, and spiritual baggage disappeared.

Here's how you can visualize this concept a bit better or even practice it, if you want. Take a small, transparent glass and fill it with water up to the brim. Now take red food coloring (you can use any food coloring – I like red because it represents pain, suffering, fatigue, negativity, fear, etc.) and put a drop in the glass. Notice how one drop changes the entire glassful of liquid. Such is life. Fear, anger, and hate can take over the substance in our lives rather quickly, if we let it. Remember the positivity ratio? Now, add a second and a third drop. Notice the color change very much? No, not at all. It's because just like in life, it's the initial fear that takes over you that is most profound and prevalent. Adding more drops does very little in terms deepening the color. Again, remember that it is easier to move from being in a positive emotional state to a negative emotional state, than it is to move from a negative emotional state to a positive emotional state.

Dump out half of your glass. What happened? You reduced the amount of red water, but did not change the consistency of it. Conventional wisdom tells us that if we reduce something, we can get rid of issues and problems. In this case, if we try to use logic, our mind will convince us that we need to remove more of the negative to make room for the positive. Using this philosophy will only reduce how much energy you have, not change the consistency. It's like a failed weight-loss program, which millions of people have encountered. They try to remove weight to get an emotional result. It doesn't work that way. We need the emotional result first, and we need a bunch of it. We need to add more positive states of consciousness to drive out the programmed, often negative states of unconsciousness.

Take darkness for example, you cannot take away darkness to make room for light. How do you get rid of it? You simply add light. Well, in the case of your life, you must add more of the three P's. Now add the metaphorical light—the three P's—by placing your glass under running water. Notice as the water refills your half empty glass, the consistency of the water doesn't change. The water is still red. Let your cup continue to fill and overflow. Notice as you continue to allow the water to enter the glass, your cup not only remains full, but it also begins to change the consistency of the water. The more water that enters the glass, the lighter the consistency (pushing out the red dye). After approximately 15 to 30 seconds of water flowing into the glass, you will see a clear glass of water. Where did all the red go? Where did all the darkness go? Where did all the fear, the pain, the anger, the hate go? It was removed by virtue of the clear water, the light, the energy, the love, the three P's. It pushed out all the red dye; it drove it out of the glass just like when you choose things that enable your positive thinking, activities which you are passionate about, and a life driven by purpose. All the baggage that holds you back will consequently be removed—and that is one of the greatest results that you can experience. Your cup, your life, is not only full, but now overflowing.

After meeting Brian and getting more involved with myTEAM TRIUMPH, all the while pursuing completion an IRONMAN, I realized just how important the three P's were in my life. Along with a few other volunteers, I was able to watch and run with Brian as he made his way those 135 miles. As part of the total event, we coordinated an American flag relay which accompanied Brian the entire way. The relay encouraged service members from all branches of the military to carry the flag for a given leg of their choosing (4 to 10 miles at a stretch). Each leg was dedicated to a service member from Wisconsin (a state in the USA) who had lost his or her life in Iraq or Afghanistan. Stephen Castner (the soldier from my unit killed in Iraq during my first deployment), along with many other brave individuals, were remembered for their ultimate sacrifice to something greater than themselves. myTEAM TRIUMPH was even able to fly Clarence Hartley (the elderly man whom I met in Boston) in to speak to our group. So many pieces of my life converged.

As I reflected during times when I carried the flag, I became extremely grateful for all that life had taught me and had brought me to that point. I realized that I could run alone, or I could run for a greater cause more profound than myself—just like Brian. Racing with athletes who had disabilities further changed my perspective on how I saw and experienced endurance events. When I ran by myself or did a triathlon by myself, I focused on time and speed. That focus played into the quality of my experience. If I did not reach the desired time, then I felt extremely discouraged, like a failure. I remember running a 10-kilometer distance (6.2 miles), finishing a few minutes slower than my goal. It made me feel angry and moved me into a negative emotional state. (Remember that drop of red dye?) I felt like a failure and turned hyper-critical of myself. I was so critical, that I missed very valuable lessons when I fell short of my time goals. I missed the fact that I could run 6.2 miles. I did not appreciate my ability. I took it for granted. When I raced with myTEAM TRIUMPH, I did not care about speed or the time it would take for us to finish a race. I simply experienced the present moment with an individual who inspired me to focus on the quality of time, rather than the quantity of time. What I finally realized was the value that each of us brought to the racing experience. As I often tell my friends, family, and colleagues, I simply provide the legs, and they provide the heart.

As I continued to learn and grow with this organization, I felt it was necessary to find an athlete afflicted with a disability who would like to do a half-iron distance triathlon with me. I became intentional in my search. The thing about intention is that, the more conscious and aware you are regarding what you want, the more likely that thing you want will manifest in your life. The person I was meant to find, I did find at the exact point in my life when I was meant to find them. Once again, everything fell into place like a jigsaw puzzle. You know those puzzles that have hundreds or thousands of pieces? Once the pieces start fitting into their right places, everything becomes clearer. The puzzle comes together, and it's no longer a mystery why certain pieces of the puzzle didn't have space.

I worked as a wellness coach at the local YMCA. I enjoyed that position very much, because it aligned with my purpose to serve others and spread the joy of health and wellness. About 2:00 p.m. on a Friday near the end of my shift, I noticed a girl sitting in a wheelchair using the functional trainer, a piece of equipment that enables the user to work most of the major muscle groups. The wheelchair didn't catch my eye; the effort she put into her workout did. She had grabbed the triceps extension bar, a V-shaped handle connected to a pulley system that lifts the weight as handle is pulled down. She sat in her chair, arms raised above her head as she pulled down on the handle with force. Extreme force! The pulley went up and down as she continued her workout.

Pulleys are interesting contraptions. Although simple in nature, they enable us to do quite complex activities, most of which result in the ability to lift more than we would be able to lift otherwise. A pulley acts as a force multiplier by increasing the amount of weight one can lift. For example, a human might have the capacity to lift 100 pounds over top their head. Let's say, for example, though, you need to lift something that weighs two hundred, three hundred or four hundred pounds. Run a rope through a pulley system (the more pulleys and ropes connected to the object, the more weight a human can lift with the same applied force). Now lifting that load becomes possible.

I often think of pulleys when I go to my father-in-law's wood shop. He collects pulleys and has them hanging all over the place: some wood, some metal; some large, and some small. They all served a purpose. To him, they still do.

As I saw the young lady in the YMCA pull that pulley with all her might, it moved me! It inspired me! I knew this was the girl I was meant to race with. I wanted to ask her if she wished to become involved with myTEAM TRIUMPH, but I feared what she'd say. I asked a coworker who said she trained this young lady to make the introduction.

"Hi, my name is Aaron," I said. I extended out my

hand.

"Hello," she said as she looked up at me from where she sat. She was a bit out of breath since she had just finished a workout set. She slowly reached out her hand and I noticed it was a bit difficult for her. So, I reached out further and we shook hands. "My name is Katie."

I smiled, wondering how to put the words together in a sentence that made sense. "Well, I work with this non-profit organization that helps athletes afflicted with disabilities compete in endurance events. I'm training for a half-iron distance triathlon that involves a 1.2-mile swim, a 56-mile bike, and a 13.1-mile run. Would you like to do that with me?"

She looked at her friend who introduced us.

"She probably thinks I'm nuts," I thought to myself.

I patiently waited as she looked back at me, then at her friend again, and then back at me.

"Crap," I thought to myself. "This was a bad idea. She'll probably say no."

"Well," she slowly said. I could tell that her mind was made up. And with a straight face, I think because she was confused by such a request, she lightly shrugged her shoulders and said, "Sure?"

That was good enough for me! I was relieved. I had been searching and praying for someone to come into my life whom I could race and build a friendship with. Little did Katie or I know that we were about to become pulleys for each other in life.

I'm sure you've used a mirror. Have you ever considered the power behind a mirror? When you look into that mirror, you see yourself in a certain way. You make judgments about yourself. Based on those judgments and the way you see yourself, you create a notion of the way you believe others see you. According to Carl Rogers, a renowned psychologist from the 20th century who used a person-centered approach, our self-concept is made up of our self-value (esteem), self-worth, and ideal self.

Self-value—or self-esteem as it's more commonly known—hinges on the value one places upon one's self as he or she experiences the world. While Rogers assumes that much of our value is derived from the experiences encountered as children, I believe that self-esteem is malleable, and, like clay, our value can be molded as the individual continues to gain and encounter more experiences that both influence and modify the personality.

Self-image consists of how we see ourselves. In the case of the mirror reflection, we draw conclusions based on what we see. That, in combination with self-esteem, can enhance or inhibit the perspective from which we choose to look and contribute to our positive or negative emotional state. Some people may categorize themselves as good or bad simply by looking at their reflections. As a health and wellness professional, I can recall many times when someone saw themselves as overweight and labeled it as a bad thing and labeled normal weight (I despise the term normal, but as per BMI standards, is what it is) as good. All in all, self-image embodies what we think, feel, and see ourselves as in the world.

Ideal self is what we aspire to be. Rogers points out that, to achieve our most ideal self and aspire to all that we have the potential to become, we must self-actualize into such a state of being.

Chapter 7:
Model for Change

Although the self-concept is composed of these three distinct ideations of the self, of the personality, I want to take a moment to address what I believe is a simple model for change. This model supports other ideas found in this book. As mentioned, Carl Rogers believes that to self-actualize, we must identify our ideal self and align our self-esteem and self-image with said ideal self. This basically states that our self-concept must be in what Rogers declares a state of congruence. I've developed a simple model, based on my experiences, which synthesize my lessons learned and knowledge in a 3-step process. I see this in all aspects of change, growth, and life. Although you may choose to adopt or reject this model, it has definitely played a significant role in my life. It goes like this:

1. Create personal awareness

This is simply a conscious choice to become enlightened, self-accepting, and self-loving of the person you already are. When it comes to weight, many people reject the fact that you, your experiences, and your entire being form a unique and wonderful thing. You aren't just a body. A body is simply the vessel that carries your personality and spirit. Your mind, your light, your spirit: that is what guides your body, which is total consciousness once you can fully understand and appreciate all that you are. You don't need to be fixed. Despite what you believe to be good or bad, successful or unsuccessful, ugly or beautiful, your body is simply a vehicle, an awesome, complex, and amazing vehicle. It's much more than any car you see on the highway. It is much more than a hunk of metal and parts that sits stationary and unused. It serves a purpose. It helps get us take action to accomplish our hopes, dreams and desires.

For example, a car, much like the human body, is a vehicle. The risk to which the vehicle is exposed depends on the driver. Consider someone who constantly texts and drives, or who drinks and drives. It is not the vehicle that puts itself at risk, but rather the vehicle's operator. In this same aspect, when your body doesn't feel up to par, it's not because the body put itself at risk. It is the mind. Your mind lives in a state of subconscious drunkenness and risk, where you have not yet achieved a state of enlightenment, respect, or healthy relationship with your body. You haven't yet connected yourself to all that you are and all that you hope to become.

Many people treat the accumulation of wealth better than they treat their bodies. They treat their vehicles better than they treat their bodies. They treat their property better than they treat their bodies. I don't mean to take away from their

92

experiences, but point out that total and complete acceptance of who you are is necessary to continue to the next step in this model.

2. Create the ideal version of yourself

This point is critical. It can, as I believe, create a sense of clarity and momentum towards all that you want for yourself, but only when it comes after total self-awareness. As I've pointed out, you'll likely realize that positivity, passion, and purpose will play some inherent role in this ideal version. I've seen many people fail—and I experienced this myself—when we create the ideal version of ourselves without complete and total awareness and acceptance of who we are. If we make this the first step in our own personal model, then it cannot be sustained because the experiences and self-concept which provide the momentum, the fuel for your vehicle, do not exist.... Yet. Take step two only once you've finished with step one. This is the most appropriate time to think about how you can incorporate and align the three P's into your life.

3. Take action

The first two steps prepare you for this final step. As easy as this step seems, you'll likely find that this third and final step is outside of everything you find comfortable. Fear, doubt, and uncertainty may creep in. That's okay. Welcome it. The more you overcome these barriers, the easier it gets.

I remember when I first got my driver's license; I

was 17 years old. When I finished my exam, I specifically remember the examiner telling me to avoid big cities because I needed a bit more practice before I could handle all the traffic and maneuvers required to safely (for myself and others) drive in that area. Well, I practiced and practiced. The more I did it, the more confident I became. The more confident I became, the more I felt like I could drive in bigger cities. This is what psychologists refer to as the confidence competence loop. The more you practice, the more competent you get. The more competent you get, the more confident you become. The more confident you become, the more you practice. And the more you practice, the more competent you become.

Taking action is grabbing competence and confidence by the horns and putting it to work for you. I've driven on the autobahn in Germany, conquered the many roundabouts in Italy, tackled some questionable driving techniques in Kuwait, and managed to weave in and out of traffic in many major U.S. cities. If my license examiner could only see me now. The point is this: once you have developed complete acceptance and appreciation for yourself and envisioned the person you want to become (using the three P's as part of the framework), then take massive and decisive action. If you fail, recognize what you have learned from that experience. Get back up and do it again.

As I previously mentioned, I developed this model as a simple way for me to continue to create awareness of who I was, who I wanted to become, and then to take action to change. You can apply this model to anything that you want for yourself, whether it's to pick up a new hobby, change careers, develop better relationships, or any other activities that add to your positive emotional state or purpose. Only you can find and decipher what will get you from where you are to where you want to be. Also, as you continue to add more and more of what you want for yourself, you'll consciously, or perhaps even subconsciously, remove that which continues to act as resistance in your life, holds you back and keeps you from becoming, changing, transcending, and self-actualizing into the person you are meant to become.

You can even place each of these steps at that point of an equilateral triangle. At the top of the triangle stands "create awareness." Along the first leg, as you begin to love, accept, and appreciate all that you are and all that you've experienced, you'll arrive at the second point, "create your ideal self." At this point of clarity, hope and belief begin to manifest in your life as you visualize the greatest and ideal version of yourself. As you move along to the second leg towards the third point, you discover that self-awareness and vision are not enough and that you must take action to become all that you want to become. As another point of emphasis, recall that, as you develop plans and actions, the three P's must be part of your action. You'll then find yourself at the third and final point, "take action." When you take action, you'll close the gap between where you were and where you want to be. You'll gain more insights, experiences, clarity, and consciousness. Don't stop. Keep moving forward. One step forward is better than any step backwards.

You might have realized that we haven't covered one leg of the triangle yet. Here's what it looks like. As you take action, you'll travel down the third and final leg. During this leg, you'll realize that, as your state of consciousness grows and expands, so does your thinking and what you believe you are capable of achieving. It is through this leg that you will arrive at complete awareness and self-love. This is what I believe to be the most basic, yet powerful, cycle of change. It's even in the form of a triangle, which just happens to be the fourth letter of the Greek alphabet–delta—which, coincidentally, means change.

The only thing certain about life is change. From the moment we are conceived until the last breath we breathe, change is constantly occurs, physically, mentally and spiritually. You can resist change or you can persist in it. You can try to stop it, which is impossible because your cells constantly change, the weather constantly changes, we constantly change. Or you can create awareness around it and use it your advantage. You can remove resistance and obtain a state of physical, mental, and spiritual flow: energy and momentum. Use the model I've provided (the delta) as your pulley to exponentially lift you, rather than limit you to live in a state of fear and unconsciousness.

Racing with Katie threw me into a whole new dimension of appreciation, consciousness, and life. As I continued to apply my change model and live the three P's, I realized the unique relationship that bonded Katie and me. After completing the first triathlon, we realized just how important each of us was to the other's growth. Katie's upbeat and positive personality, despite perceived limits, gave me a unique perspective on life. As I continued to suffer my body through bouts of physical fatigue and exhaustion, she, in turn, got to experience the joy of endurance racing. I believe that I benefitted from our relationship more than she did. Our time together completely changed my entire outlook on life and enhanced meaningfulness of living with positivity, passion, and purpose. I'll never forget her reply when someone asked her what she felt when we raced together. Her answer: "Freedom."

As I write this, it sends chills down my spine. I deeply appreciate the opportunities and experiences we built together that helped me remove resistance in life—the light which drove out so much of the darkness from my past. After our half-iron experience, the first race we ever did together, we both realized that we wanted more. We wanted to push harder and further than we thought we were capable of. My endurance racing took on a completely new form. I came to the conclusion one night that IRONMAN was not meant to be my journey, but our journey, one that we must take together.

Get ready, because here comes another jigsaw puzzle moment. Everything timed out perfectly and fell into a unique sequence precisely when it was supposed to. Taking on an IRONMAN requires a lot of preparation, especially for an athlete that has never done one before. In 2012, after volunteering for IRONMAN Wisconsin at the finishers chute in early September (which was necessary to gain priority to register for the race in 2013), I realized that I wanted to attempt an IRONMAN with Katie. While on my second deployment, I watched a video about a father and son, Rick and Dick Hoyt. In the video, I saw Dick swimming. After a couple seconds, the camera panned out to him pulling a raft with his son, Rick, in it. Combined with some uplifting music, the video moved me to tears as Dick pushed and pulled his son through an IRONMAN triathlon. It was one of the greatest examples of love that I had ever seen. It moved me, as I'm sure it's moved many other people. Despite being in a stressful environment away from all my family and friends, this video brought me a sense of peace.

After Katie and I completed a half iron distance race, I knew that we could complete an IRONMAN. It was time to remove all the resistance and create momentum.

After signing up for IRONMAN in 2013, which I was scheduled to do alone, I reached out to Christian Jensen, the Executive Director for myTEAM TRIUMPH. I told him about my desire to race with Katie. Unfortunately, Christian explained to me that he was actually in conversation with IRONMAN for him to assist an athlete through the race, and that they were only going to give one entry to the organization. It crushed me to learn that, because of the mental preparation and courage it took to convince myself that I was capable of completing a race of this magnitude with Katie.

Since I was still in the military, I had been selected

for a promotion that would require training at a different location in the country. This training would occur in early September, during the exact time that I was to complete IRONMAN Wisconsin. I was able to push my registration to the following year. I wasn't disappointed because I knew that I now had another shot to do IRONMAN with Katie. I didn't wait.

As soon as I transferred my registration, I contacted Christian to let him know, and to ask if they allow a team to compete the following year and that Katie and I be considered. He said that we would be first on the list. As the months passed and Katie and I continued to race together, Christian and I would reconnect every once in a while to see if IRONMAN had made a decision.

"Unfortunately, they haven't," he explained. "We've received some interest from other athletes as well. We're still waiting to confirm how many spots we'll get."

I inquired as to the other athletes seeking entry. I only recognized one, Adam Lofquist. During that time, Adam and I challenged ourselves to a 50-mile running race in the Door County peninsula, a beautiful and challenging course stretching down the thumb of northeast Wisconsin. We ran that race together, or should I say struggled through that race together. It was challenging, but reinforced why I believe that running for the quality of building relationships trumped running for the quantity of time. I reached out to Adam once I found out that he wanted to do IRONMAN as well. I decided that if he were not able to compete in the race by assisting a disabled athlete as their own team, then he could race with Katie and I on our team. It felt like the right thing to do, mostly because myTEAM TRIUMPH is not about the individual experience, but about relationship building. So, if I was to make it only about me and my experience with Katie, then that would have been a pretty selfish thing to do. Just like a jigsaw puzzle piece falling right into place, that's exactly what happened. myTEAM TRIUMPH only received one team entry into IRONMAN Wisconsin in 2014. As such, it would be something that Katie, Adam, and I would tackle together.

Training for IRONMAN was extremely challenging. I had just graduated from college with a degree in health promotion and wellness and was in the middle of changing jobs and finishing up some required resident military courses clear on the other side of the USA. Life was out of balance. However, I had the energy, momentum, and desire to continue to push further. The better trained my body became, the more physical, mental, and spiritual energy I received.

To put in perspective the energy required to push and pull an adult human being through a 2.2-mile swim, a 112-mile bike, and 26.2-mile run, it's about thirty to forty percent greater, depending on the terrain. For example, I could bike approximately an average of about 20 miles per hour comfortably on flat terrain. When we hook up the trailer to the bike, it's a struggle to average 14 miles per hour. The IRONMAN that we were about to experience, has one of the hilliest bike courses in their racing circuit. Some of the hills were so steep that I had a hard time getting up them by myself while on some individual training rides without Katie.

She's not a heavy person, but pulling her up in a trailer attached to my bike made it extremely difficult. In the easiest gear, the lowest resistance, I could barely turn over the pedals. But it didn't matter. Even though my heart rate would push borderline to my maximum for my age, we always kept moving forward. My training, just like my life, was not balanced. I volunteered where I could, worked when I must, trained when I had time. I realized that my life didn't need balance; it needed energy. When I put more energy in, especially when they involved living the three P's, I became more energized. I had more clarity. I had more momentum. At this point, based on my experiences and my lifestyle philosophy and the success I've personally witnessed and researched from others, most don't have balance, they have momentum.

This next point will challenge everything you know. Think about society's pressure to pursue a state of balance. I believe that working towards a state of balance denies the physics of what makes us physically, mentally, and spiritually extraordinary. That overemphasis has surrendered us to extreme mediocrity, which isn't necessarily a bad thing. It just creates less opportunity to find and live the three P's, to experience a present state of consciousness, and use the delta (the triangle to change) to self-actualize and live up to our potential. You hear it all the time, every day, everywhere: you must find balance, because being in a state of balance allows you to feel good, feel better, feel peace.

What if that thinking actually added more resistance in your life? Resistance that was keeping you from a unique and exciting human experience? I see it all too often. If you are busy, you must remove things in your life and replace them with the things that matter. Remember the drop of red dye in the water glass? Removing something from your life doesn't take the "red" or the undesired feeling away. I understand the intention behind balance. We want people to feel like they have a sense of control over their lives. We want them to feel like they have more energy in life. But the flaw in that thinking rests on the perceptions of others. When someone thinks about having more energy, it typically means, that one must remove stressors that take away and drain your energy in life. All of which is based on perception.

According to Statistic Brain, some of the biggest stressors in life are job pressure, money, health, relationships, poor nutrition, media overload, and sleep deprivation. If only we worked less, made more money, had better health, better relationships, ate healthfully, spent less time on our devices, and slept more, then we could likely reduce stress and achieve a state of balance. As a result, we'd have less stress and more energy. But many of us live in a state of subconsciousness, of automatic and programmed thinking. We don't resort to things that give us balance or energy. A job provides money, yet it's the number two stressor in the USA; and the money we earn from our jobs contributes to the quality of personal relationships. Relationships often suffer a great deal of stress when there is a lack of money.

Stress activates a portion of the brain called the amygdala, and results in a fight or flight response which constricts blood vessels and increases heart rate and blood pressure. Chronically speaking, stress experienced over long periods of time, can reduce immune system function and make an individual susceptible to heart disease and other stress-related chronic health conditions. Stress can also inhibit certain pathways in the brain that block the connection to your prefrontal cortex, the area of the brain responsible for making sound judgments. Furthermore, stress can lead to poor sleep habits. Then, to incorporate more balance in life, we go on vacation, which takes money. We watch television, which takes money. We buy new smart phones, cars or houses. We do things that cost money to try and restore the balance in our lives. Stress adds resistance to our lives. It takes away our health and well-being and keeps us from thinking clearly and sleeping adequately. We seem to believe however, that we must spend money to have more balance. But spending money reduces how much money you actually have—which contributes to even greater stress. This systematic and cyclical thinking about balance can add surmounting emotional resistance to the three P's.

To make more money, what must you do? You must put more energy into an activity, whether self-education, starting a new business, picking up another job, or getting a degree. If you were to take one of these paths, I would argue that it is going to require a substantial amount of energy.

Let's say for a moment, that as a result of making a bit more money, you develop a sense of security, a sense of freedom. I'm not saying that money is the solution to all your problems. I'm simply stating that if you seek balance, get ready because that decision might lead to mediocre choices that will only add to your stress, not take it away. What if an extra two hours each night spent learning or working on a business earned you an extra $15,000 per year? What could you do with that? How would that influence the stresses you have in life? Look at people who are achieving what you want to achieve. Do you think they have a sense of balance? I'd argue no. They are probably knee-deep every single day pursuing a life filled with positivity, passion and purpose. Their schedules aren't balanced. Their heads are barely above the water and it feels great!

Think about success stories such as Abraham Lincoln, the son of a poor farmer who became president of the United States; Benjamin Franklin, an apprentice destined to take over the family business as a candle maker who discovered electricity and signed the Declaration of Independence; Wilbur and Orville Wright, two good 'ol boys from Ohio who did not graduate from high school, yet invented a machine that transformed civilization with powered flight; or Henry Ford who was told that a V-6 engine was impossible to create, yet he did. Albert Einstein, Bill Gates, Helen Keller, Steve Jobs, Mother Theresa, Mark Zuckerberg, the list goes on and on. Do you think that these individuals had a state of balance? Probably not. On the contrary, they had momentum; and, as I continued to make headway seeking more momentum in life much like these individuals, I realized that pursuing balance only held me back.

Achieving all that I wanted in life, which included living with the three P's, required that I think, speak, and act in a way that gave me more energy, more momentum. One need not look very far to see how it works. Think of it like a bicycle. If you simply get onto a bicycle and try to balance yourself, it's nearly impossible. As soon as you lift your feet onto the pedals, if you don't move forward at all, it's highly probable that you will fall over. But, once you start pedaling, something amazing happens. With a little practice, the momentum keeps you upright so that you can continue to pedal and move forward. The more you pedal, the easier it gets to stay upright and the less risk there is of falling over.

It's amazing how a few rotations on the pedal can crank and turn your wheels to take you further than if you simply stayed at rest. Once the momentum's there—once the energy is there—you can ride that for a while before having to crank the pedals again. Such is life. When you push down on the pedals of positivity, passion, and purpose, it creates more momentum which allows you to stay upright longer. As you move from the person you are to the person you want to become, it creates experiences and opportunities for you to learn and grow. It's forward and progressive. With more momentum comes more courage, confidence (which influences your self-concept), awareness, and hope.

Quit pedaling your bike and momentum, at some point, will cease, just like in life. If you stop, consciously or subconsciously, applying force to the three P's into life—which are the pedals that create momentum—and choose to coast, at some point your energy will run out. Hence, you will stop and eventually fall over. It's simple physics.

Newton's First Law of Motion states that "An object at rest stays at rest, unless acted on by an unbalanced force. An object in motion continues in motion with the same speed and in the same direction, unless acted on by an unbalanced force." A balanced force, for the purpose of this analogy, is defined as when two forces of equal magnitude push in opposite directions. If you take a book and set it on the floor, what would happen? It would stay at rest. A state of balance. Two opposing forces keep it still. The first force is gravity, which pushes down on the object; the second force is the surface on which the object rests. The floor, along with the earth, pushes up against gravity. Now with your hand, push against the book. What happens? Since you applied force, which was unbalanced, and because the force from your hand was greater than the air surrounding the object, the book moves. However, because of the combined force of gravity pushing down, the earth pushing up (which is balanced), and the friction of the floor (which is resistance), the object will stop. The momentum it once had will cease. It will no longer move forward. How do you get it to move again? You apply more unbalanced force.

In life, applying an unbalanced force is like overflowing your cup filled with red-dyed water with the three P's. It removes the resistance (friction) and pushes you forward in life (unbalanced force). However, you must keep applying the force to keep the energy up and the momentum moving forward. Opposite forces, which I believe to be those that bring us to a negative emotional state, will act as a point of resistance. The only way to fight your way through and keep your momentum is to continue to use the change model outlined in the previous chapter (awareness, ideal self, and action). Perspective is what will determine the state of mind that you allow yourself to apply force, and create sustainable momentum. As you practice having a positive perspective, you will begin to change the context of your thinking. The more you practice changing your thinking, the better you get.

Neurplasticity is the molding and reshaping of your neural connections, thoughts, attitudes, behaviors, and choices. As your thoughts and perspectives change, your brain physiologically and psychologically transforms so that it is no longer a book, but a ball. Now consider this, with the same amount of unbalanced force for each object (the book and ball), which goes further? Right, the ball. Finding the right perspective will help optimize how you see yourself, how you see others, and how you see the world. It will help you mold your mind into the object to overcome resistance generate perpetual momentum.

Since I quit drinking, many people have asked me why I stopped. Some even criticize me for being sober: "You should have a beer and loosen up." "You can have a drink. You always used to drink.

What happened?" I recognized that alcohol, for me, created resistance (friction in my life).

These critical statements affected me on a personal level. They stressed me out and made me wonder if other people saw me or thought of me this way. It slowed my momentum for a short time. I even considered drinking again, which might have made me more socially acceptable. Then I realized that my perspective was garbage and I needed to take out the trash.

I've come to know and understand how important perspective is in life. It can help create the momentum and unbalanced force necessary to move you forward. It embodies all that you see, think, feel, and ultimately experience. When applied, it can create a surreal state of consciousness, appreciation, gratitude, and love. For example, someone who dislikes their job, but has the appreciation for the money they make to put food on the table has a positive perspective. Someone who dislikes the car they drive or the home she lives in, but has the perspective to appreciate that she can get from place to place or have a roof over her head has a positive perspective.

Racing with Katie has given me valuable perspective and awareness that not everyone can run, bike, or swim. Now when I race, I appreciate that I am able to do those things, because there are people in this world who wish, perhaps only for a day, that they could do those things. With that awareness, I create my ideal self and take action (the delta change model) to create momentum in my life.

I've met a lot of resistance since my epiphany and the day when I self-transcended into positivity, passion, and purpose. Just like the person who criticized me for not drinking, so others have criticized me for pursuing my passions, telling me that I would likely fail. All that emotional baggage and negativity pushed against me, tried to slow me down. I came to realize that if I focus on myself and put the right things in my life, much like the continuous flow of water into a cup filled with red-dyed water, it will continue to energize me, give me momentum, and get me closer to my hopes, dreams, and aspirations. Therefore, if you feel constantly tired, fatigued, stressed, or in a negative emotional state, I'm going to challenge you to seek those things that energize you. Focus less on balance and more on momentum. Appreciate your hustle. Appreciate your hard work and effort. Align it with the three P's until you become a ball moving forward with tons of unstoppable and ever-progressing momentum.

Use the change process and incorporate the three P's into your life until your energy overflows and pushes out all the anger, greed, fear, and negative self-concept. I'm not suggesting that you simply fill your life with stuff. We already do that with our busy and hectic schedules. Our busy lives full of stuff, which doesn't fill us up, is exactly what drives us to seek balance. It's what keeps us complacent. Keep that momentum going, just like when riding a bike, so that even if you slow down, you never stop. Because the point at which you stop, the point at which you only pursue balance is the point that you fall over.

Chapter 8:
Time Organization

As I trained for IRONMAN, I realized that balance would only hold me back from all that was necessary in my life: 4:00 a.m. wake-ups, work, family time, and volunteer activities. Every day was filled with activities that contributed to my positive emotional state and with passions that helped me achieve my purpose. The more momentum I achieve in my life (by adding the three P's), the more energy and less resistance I had. The more I practiced doing the things that gave me energy, the better I got, the easier things got, the more momentum I got.

There were weeks when I had to commit to twenty hours of IRONMAN training. I continued to increase my personal awareness around momentum. I became really good at recognizing things that multiplied my energy, rather than divided my energy. I came to understand that time wasn't against me, it was for me. It was a gift that was given to me every single day. I saw and heard so much of society say, "I don't have time," which in all honesty, was something I often said prior to my lack of understanding. Just like anything in life, it was intertwined with my body, mind, and spirit. We existed in a relationship.

Time is not money. Time is value. Benjamin Franklin once said, "Dost thou love life? Then do not squander time, for that's the stuff life is made of."

Time is energy. It is momentum. It is freedom and it appreciates as we age. Remember when you were a kid and you couldn't wait to become an adult? Now that you're an adult, do you wish time would just slow down? I sometimes feel that way, that time would slow down, mostly because I find so much value in this world and the time that I have here.

I love meeting new people, challenging myself and experiencing life. As I continue to age, just like everyone else, my time becomes more valuable. Therefore, I need to make choices that perpetuate more energy, more freedom Consequently, I can do the things I want to create even more value for myself and this world. Time is something that is both finite and infinite. Your physical life operates on a certain rhythm that, at some point, will stop.

Place your hand over your heart. Feel that beating, that rhythm. The human heart beats around 118,000 times per day, and over 3 billion times throughout the average lifespan. In that aspect. Time is finite. Each time your heart beats, you get closer to certain death. I don't using this as a scare tactic, but rather as a way to create awareness of the value your heart and time have in life. Time will continue once you are gone. It is within that span where time is infinite. It won't end. Each second, minute, hour, and day you spend here on this earth becomes an opportunity to self-actualize and live up to your potential. Most of us see time as a quantifiable, objective unit of measure. When you realize that time is subjective and holds a certain qualitative value, that's when you can use the three P's and the change process in a way that creates more momentum and more energy. Rather than balancing time, as an objective and quantitative measure and point of subconscious and programmed thinking, use it to create more momentum and energy. I've devised a three-tier, hierarchy value of time. It works like this:

Quantitative – Some people see time as a matter of seconds, hours, and days. They are not consciously aware of the experience that life brings and often overlook the lessons one learns day-to-day. This level of time exists on the lowest tier.

Qualitative – This perspective looks beyond the quantity of time and recognizes the energy that flows from an experience. They are in tune with their conscious choice and take advantage of opportunities that contribute to a positive emotional state. This level of time moves upwards to the middle of the tier.

Experiential – This is the most present state of consciousness, where all the senses are used to recognize the value in everything in our physical and metaphysical life. It transcends us as creatures who have meaning and purpose on earth. The experiential perception is the arrival of self-actualization, where positivity, passion, and purpose (the three P's) converge at the core of your being and existence. This level of time is the pinnacle of the three-tier hierarchy.

For example, I could watch TV for an hour (the

average American watches five hours per day), which is sixty minutes (quantitative) that will likely leave me with the same amount of energy. I could go for a run by myself for sixty minutes (qualitative), where I would get more energy (because when you exercise, you get more energy). Or I could go for a run with Katie (experiential) for sixty minutes, and as a result, will exponentially increase my energy and momentum as I live with the three P's. You can use this hierarchy of time in any aspect of life, as it directly relates to the relationships you have in life.

If you don't make time for something, what happens to it? It decreases in value and ultimately dies if you avoid it too long. Think about marriage: if you don't put time into the relationship, how can it last? It likely won't. Think about food: if you don't put time into making your meals, what are you going to eat? Fast food? If you eat fast food, how does that add to all that you want for yourself in life? Whereas taking an extra ten minutes in your day to make lunch could create the energy and momentum necessary to do more of the things you want in life.

I see this all too often in many organizations I've worked with or worked in. Many employees see time as quantitative. They begin their work day at 8:00 a.m., for example, and don't stop working until 5:00 p.m. They eat lunch at their desk and only get up if they have to go to the bathroom or attend a meeting. Research shows that the brain can only handle about ninety minutes to two hours of straight focus. This rhythm is pre-wired into our brains. Anything longer than that leads to decreased levels of productivity. It's amazing what five minutes of time away from your desk (qualitative) can do to create more momentum, energy, and focus on your work. According to the Draugiem Group, following a recently conducted study using a computer application to track employees' work habits, in a typical 8-hour work day, those who take breaks are going to be more productive in a day than those who don't. As you begin to use the time you are given each day to incorporate the 3 P's, you'll realize the greater sense of energy, vitality, and momentum you have in life.

Time is not created equal in this aspect. Think of it as if it were money you were to invest and the compound interest that would accrue. There is a unique relationship that exists if you invest your money when you are younger. If you invest $100 every month when you are twenty years old, with an annual interest rate of seven percent, your money would appreciate and grow to be over $240 thousand by the time you are sixty. Now take that same $100 monthly investment and annual interest rate, except start at age forty-five, and it will grow to only$30 thousand by the time you are sixty. Much like an investment made earlier in life, time becomes an energy multiplier the more you continue to invest in yourself and work towards a life of positivity, passion, and purpose. As you continue to develop a healthy relationship with time, you'll no longer use it as something that disables you or as an excuse. You'll find that time enables you to experience all that life has to offer: love, joy, peace, and power.

How can you use your time to exponentially increase your energy and momentum, which will reduce fatigue and stress? Here's my secret formula. First, draw a circle and place a dot in the middle. This represents your day. In this circle, you will allocate your time, by specifically doing what gives you energy first and foremost. So, what is one of the single most important activities you do each day that contributes to your energy and total well-being? If you said sleep, you're right. Getting the right amount of sleep is imperative for good energy and health. Experts recommend adults get seven to nine hours of sleep per night. With that recommendation means you will likely spend about 30 percent of your life sleeping. Base your day around your sleep schedule.

I use sleep as the starting point because fatigue from lack of sleep can decrease performance, and, over long periods of time, health. Sleep helps your body recover and rejuvenate itself. Deprivation of sleep can increase your risk of developing high blood pressure, heart disease, and stroke. I use this statement not to prevent death, but to promote life. When you feel energized and invigorated, you can add emotional compounding interest into your life! Why not use sleep to your advantage, so you can do the things you want to do for longer?

Learn the least amount of time in those recommended seven to nine hours that leaves you feeling energized and ready to conquer the day. For me, eight hours is the most optimal; however, I can perform exceptionally well at seven hours of sleep, especially when I incorporate the three P's in my daily life. So, create and draw two lines from the middle of the circle that accounts for the 7-9 hours of sleep in your day. Now subtract that number from 24 (so since I sleep about 7 hours per night, 24-7= 14). Next, think about an activity that gives you energy just simply by thinking about it. This should be a passion or something that aligns with your purpose. Maybe it's meditating, exercising, reading, or writing. Whatever it is, make sure it invigorates your soul. Now take 10 percent of the hours that you are awake and allocate that time to do the thing(s) which gives you energy (14 x 10% = 1.4 hours). You can break this time up throughout the day, or do it all at once. Whatever it is, this is the minimum amount of time you must use to focus on your three P's. If you find yourself starting to make an excuse, "But Aaron, I just don't have the time to do this," reappraise the value of time (or go through the change model presented earlier) and recognize that all we're doing here is adding more clear water to the red-dyed water—in essence, more awareness.

Allocating 10 percent of your day towards the three P's will force (unbalanced force) you to reconsider the value of time and result in exponentially more energy. I like to do my minimum 1.4 hours of self-growth and three P's application right when I wake up. It reduces the risk of valeity so I can avoid procrastination and take the third step in the change model: take action. Once you've charted out your sleep and the minimum 10 percent of the remaining hours focused on the three P's, you may now fill in all the other tasks you must accomplish each day. Work, school, errands, whatever you have going on in life: now you can fill those in. I recommend keeping a journal to log your experiences as you put this activity into practice. This is the technique that I used during my IRONMAN training and which I continue to use in everyday life. It's helped me create more clarity and commitment to myself as I work towards more energy, momentum, and growth.

I'll never forget waking up the morning of IRONMAN. It was fresh and cool outside. I could hardly sleep the night before. I was so full of energy, focused, and ready to challenge my mind and body! You wouldn't have believed I was only going on about four hours of sleep. I couldn't help it. Thoughts of race day kept going through my mind, some fear, some doubt. Did I train enough for this? Will my body endure seventeen hours of intense physical and mental activity? What if we fail? What if we don't make the cutoff points for each leg? (Quick side note: IRONMAN places cutoff times for the swim, bike, and run.) They must not have received the memo about time being qualitative or experiential. My biggest worry, in this case, was the bike. We had roughly about 8.5 hours to complete the bike, based on how quickly we finished the swim. We figured about one hour and forty minutes to swim the 2.4-mile first leg. That meant we needed to achieve a 13.2 miles-per-hour average on the bike to finish before the cutoff. As mentioned earlier, it was a struggle to achieve a 14 mile-per-hour average with Katie; with all of the hills on this course, we knew we had our work cut out for us. I'm reminded of a quote from the Bible that became my philosophy for this race and even more so in life:

> *And not only that, but we also boast in our sufferings knowing that suffering produces endurance, and endurance produces character, and character produces hope, and hope does not disappoint us... (Romans 5:3–5)*

What this verse tells me is that all that I had experienced kept leading me to something better, something greater. In the case of IRONMAN, I realized that it was not just the event that was about to change me, but rather the process leading up to the event. You can apply this on a grander scale, because life, in and of itself, is a process. A process of change. A process of growth. A process of learning. A process of understanding. A process of love. A process of failure. A process of character development. A process of finding hope. A process of self-actualizing into our greatest and most authentic selves. Again, this happens once we have the insight, awareness (the first step in the change model), and acceptance that everything you've encountered up to this point was meant for you. It's part of your destiny. Part of your purpose. Part of your being and very existence.

Perhaps, because you, like me, lived in a state of subconsciousness and relied on what the world said you should be, how you should think, act and feel, you failed to realize the beauty, uniqueness, and perfection in all that you already are.

I remember two significant instances with some clients. Both wanted to lose weight. The first was a middle-aged woman, approximately forty years old and about three hundred pounds. Conventional wisdom based on standard BMI would tell you that, relative to her height, she was considered morbidly obese, a medical term that associates obesity with increased relative risk of dying prematurely. Our culture sees people like this and, in a nutshell, demands they change or die. When love informs our message and governs the way we communicate that message, it is not only better received, but comforting because people feel supported. Compare this to fear underlying that message, which contributes to feelings of inadequacy, labeling, and poor self-concept.

I was a victim of poor self-concept. I don't blame others, but societal pressures to achieve a certain body image flooded my mind. I couldn't love myself or invest the necessary time in myself, because I didn't have a healthy relationship with myself. At the lowest points in my life, I ate fast food twice a day. Combined with all the alcohol, I was considered borderline obese. When I finally decided to go to the gym, I tried working towards having a ripped six-pack and large chest. I spent over $300 per month on supplements chasing this body type. After learning more about myself and my body, I came to realize that I was working towards a body that society said I should have, not what I thought I should have.

Who should take away my experience as a human being? The answer: no one. I'm happy to report that I don't have a six pack or a big chest. My arms are a measly fourteen inches and I'm down thirty-five pounds from my highest weight ever. But that is only because I developed a healthy concept of myself. I continued to fill my cup with the three P's, and all the exercise I did, which represented a commitment to myself, forced (unbalanced force) me to lose weight.

When I met this woman who was close to three hundred pounds, I couldn't help but realize her uniqueness. Beyond BMI categorization, beyond what the world (through dogma) sees her as, I saw a person who was already enough. As we continued our sessions and as she searched for her meaning in life, she told me that she had bad teeth growing up. Because she didn't take care of them, she felt she couldn't smile. My heart sank. Can you imagine not smiling for twenty years? A smile feeds and nourishes your soul with an energy of light that reflects all the happiness and positive emotional states you feel. It is an expression of love. How can you feel whole or complete without this gift? Well, in her words, "You can't!"

A few months later, while doing some wellness coaching for the Army, I met a man who entered a program for soldiers who fail to meet or maintain height and weight standards. As we continued to talk, he expressed concern about some things he was dealing with. He had been deployed three times and suffered turmoil and loss during each deployment. He developed post-traumatic stress. He explained that he had severe flashbacks when he exercised. Relative to his traumatic encounters while deployed, exercising increased his heart rate and adrenaline, which triggered a flashback episode.

Here are two cases of people with psychological

121

turmoil who "need" to lose weight, stricken by experiences in life which keep them from transcending into their fullest potential. Is it fair to pass judgment on these two cases and say, well if they really wanted to, they could? I think such judgment is prejudicial to the good of humanity. It reduces us to our lowest state of being, of functioning: a state of fear, dogma and unconsciousness. Here's the reality: people go through tough things every single day. As they continue to pursue a life filled with positivity, passion, and purpose, they don't need you to be another barrier in their way. What they need is for you to be their opportunity. As such, we need to empathize with people when we want to criticize; we need to forgive when we want to be bitter: and, we need to empower when we want to gossip.

I understand, those might be very hard things to do, because it goes against conventional wisdom and possibly all the challenges you've come to know. But here's the deal: easy choices are often those that keep you from growing, because strength is a product of making hard choices. There is always more to a person than what's merely apparent. All criticizing does is bring to life exactly what we internally experience. And likely, because we cannot accept and love ourselves (part of the first step of change), we cannot accept and love others.

If you search for the bad in people, you'll find it. If you search for the good in people, you'll find it. Find time each day to seek out that which is good in life. Doing so will open your mind to what truly matters in life and give you a greater perspective on the blessings that continue to manifest. Make a conscious choice to not react with anger. Search your feelings to understand what drives this emotion (step 1 awareness), decide what emotional state of mind you'd rather have (step 2 – create ideal self), and then constructively take action (step 3 – take action).

As I've pointed out, emotions are extremely powerful because they influence the choices we make. Consequently, you'll notice extreme differences in the outcomes if you act from love, rather than fear. Our world needs the best of you every day, and you deserve to have the best of the world every day. I try to give the world the best of me whenever I can.

As we made our way out into the water, I became extremely focused. Everything in my life had prepared me for this journey that Katie, Adam, and I were about to take together. The starting line stood about two hundred meters from shore. As we slowly made our way out, self-acceptance and self-love engulfed me. I had done all that I could, training-wise, to get me to this point. My body was going to hurt and my mind was going to tell me to quit; but, my will to win, to keep moving forward, to keep the momentum, carried far more value (experiential time) than the fear of missing the approximately 8.5-hour bike and 17-hour total race cutoffs (quantitative). With the boat that carried Katie attached to my waist and Adam at my side, we were ready. We were meant for this day. As we waited for the starter gun to go off, other athletes clung to the boat. We talked about how the day was going to pan out and many of them wished Katie good luck. The shot fired and we were off.

Something you should know about me is that when it comes to swimming, there's little difference between me and a rock. Neither of us floats or swims very well. I developed a fear of swimming with my head in the water when I was a kid. The swimming instructor told me to jump in the deep end and that he would catch me. I did and he didn't. I could not keep myself afloat. I coughed up water for a couple of minutes. It's one of the few memories I can recall at the age of four and the one responsible for my negative relationship with water. Sure, I went to the swimming pool and had fun, but I had an intense fear of swimming with my head under water in the deep end.

After I made the choice to live with positivity, passion and purpose, and to complete an IRONMAN, I figured I'd have to learn how to swim a freestyle stroke. That meant confronting my fears. What I learned, as I became more conscious of my life and the power behind my thinking, was that my belief drove my attitude and my attitude drove my effort. Because I believed that I was afraid of swimming and couldn't put my head in the water, I had a negative attitude towards putting my head in the water. And because I had a negative attitude of putting my head in the water (we make choices based more on emotion than logic), I put no effort into trying to do so. I simply accepted that I could never do it. As a result of this belief, I never tried.

I used this concept to my advantage. I told myself that it was possible for me to do this. As soon as I thought this, I changed a belief from impossible to possible. Along with that, my attitude followed. I now had a better attitude towards swimming. Because I was more positive in my attitude, I put more effort into it. With a lot of practice (remember the competence/confidence loop?), I came to appreciate swimming. It became a spiritual representation of conquering fear, and I now love it! You can take this concept and apply it to whatever you want for yourself in your life.

Think about it: do you believe you can sail around the world? What is your attitude towards this belief? How much effort are you going to put into it? I recently watched a documentary on Netflix called The Maidentrip. I love documentaries. I found that if I want to watch TV for an hour (quantitative time), then I would get more out of a documentary (qualitative) than I would watching a sitcom, drama, or other show.

In this documentary, Laura Dekker, a 14-year-old Dutch girl traveled around the world on her boat. The youngest individual to ever accomplish such a feat, she stated, "As soon as I get on my boat, something inside me changes. Then I really feel what living is." Did Dekker have to believe in herself and her abilities? Yes, and, because that belief changed something inside her (positive emotion), she put effort into doing it. Okay, now that I've provided an over-the-top and around-the-world example, let's take a look at our own lives.

Do you believe that you can incorporate ten minutes a day investing in yourself? When I pose this question to audiences or clients, the typical response is, "Yes, that's easy." As soon as you begin to believe, think, and speak those words, you begin to move into a positive emotional state, one which influences your attitude. How much effort could you put into only ten minutes of self-improvement each day? I usually get a lot of head nods at this point in agreement. Some even say, "I could do that."

Well, it doesn't stop there. You must believe, as I do in you, that you are capable beyond measure. Your life is the most valuable form of treasure. Let no one break you. Let nothing overtake you. Let joy shake you. Let love make you. Leave the worst of you in the past because the best of you is coming in fast. You'll find that, in the end, if you have the will to win, then greatest version of yourself that there has ever been. Belief drives your attitude and attitude drives your effort. As you review all that we've learned so far, consider what you've believed that will work for you in your life. That will likely indicate what you will put effort into. Don't be afraid to start there. This is what I believe to be a phenomenal guide for anyone looking to change their life (or organization).

The steps and learnings from this book are important in the order listed. But, as I've pointed out, I'd rather you take one concept and implement it into your life than avoid it altogether. When you believe in something, when you value something, that's when the effort comes. As you continue to make the choice to implement the three P's into your life, use the delta (model of change), see time as a valuable resource that provides extraordinary experiences, and continue to increase momentum, then you will see your life unfold into a new light which drives away the darkness and leaves your glass filled with crystal clear water.

After finishing the swim course, we made it into transition and changed as quickly as we could to make sure we had as much time as possible to complete the 112-mile bike before the cutoff. Adam started first on the bike. We had a meticulous plan to get Katie to the finish line that used our individual strengths to our collective advantage. I would pull her the entire swim (because switching mid-swim amid thousands of other swimmers was a bad idea), I would take 60 percent of pulling her on the bike with the major hills, since I had a bike strength (Adam would take the other 40 percent), and Adam would take 60 percent of the run, since that was his strength (and I would take the other 40 percent). During the bike portion specifically, we planned to switch who pulled Katie about six times over the 8.5 hours, knowing that each time we switched we lost time. Leading up to our IRONMAN race, Katie, Adam and I practiced making the switch on our trailer hitches, so, when race day came, we could do it as quickly and efficiently as possible (remember the competence confidence loop?). We were like a pit crew on a NASCAR circuit; but, instead of switching out tires, we were switching Katie's chair onto each other's trailer hitch. During the bike, the weather grew increasingly hot. One particular hill that stood at an incredibly steep incline, one of the steepest hills I'd ever seen. While preparing for our IRONMAN, Adam and I trained on these hills with Katie. The hill was so steep that we could not pedal up it, we had to push Katie to the top. Getting up the hill was one fear on my mind prior to the race. Because the bike course does two loops for a certain number of miles, I had to do this hill twice. I had never pulled Katie up this hill. The last time we tried, we failed.

As I approached the hill, I tried to pick up speed and momentum (simple physics, remember). I remember seeing a blur of people on both sides. I imagine that's what Tour de France athletes feel like. People—what I could see from my periphery—lined the street, shouting, cheering, all while running next to us as we gave that hill all we had! I didn't focused on them; I focused on what was in front of me. That's all I could see. It's all I wanted to see. I made this hill a representation of all the crap that I had gone through in life. As I climbed it, I released it into the world, never to feel ashamed of the choices I made, but to see them as necessary because they brought me to this point. About half-way up the hill, I noticed myself getting a little lightheaded. My feet barely turned the pedals over. It was the slowest I could go without falling over. I was seated for the first half of the hill to focus on efficiency. I wondered if I would make the top. I didn't know if my body could handle the heat. The fact that I was pulling Katie up that monster of a hill didn't make it any easier for me.

Adam and I used our strengths, but I did not mention that Katie used her strength to help me. Katie was the voice of inspiration. She was the bridge that connected us to each other and to the purpose behind our doing this in the first place. Her presence amplified the positivity, multiplied the passion, and clarified the purpose. When I needed her strength most, she spoke, "Keep going, Aaron, you can do it." As the words make their way into this book I still feel the rush, the drive, the inspiration, the motivation, everything inside me converging. I stood out of my seat. I cranked down on those pedals. I refused to stop. I was only moving one direction, and that was forward! We reached the top of that hill twice that day, not because we worried about our weaknesses, but because we focused on our strengths, which is what teamwork is all about. That is what helps make people successful.

We hear it all too often. Your weaknesses are "X," or you need to do a better job doing "Y." That methodology is wrong. I'll start with a quote from one of my mentors, David Rendall, author of *The Freak Factor*: Discovering Uniqueness by Flaunting Weakness. He says, "What makes you weird makes you wonderful. And what makes you weak also makes you strong." What I realized when racing with Katie is that we both had perceived weaknesses. Trying to fix those weaknesses only reduces your corresponding strengths. Rendall makes a very similar point and references messy people (perceived weakness) who have corresponding strengths of creativity. To "fix" a weakness only reduces one's corresponding strengths. If an artist were to become meticulously organized, it would likely reduce their creativity. Trying to fix weaknesses is one of the most inefficient things one can spend time on.

Preparing for IRONMAN, I focused on my strengths and let Katie and Adam worry about enhancing their strengths. We didn't focus on our perceived weaknesses. It's in those perceived weaknesses that there are corresponding strengths. Amplify your strengths, especially when it comes to living the three P's, and you will energize, magnify, and multiply—exponentially— everything in your life. Besides, who likes to listen to a litany of their inadequacies? That can lead to a negative emotional state.

Don't get me wrong. I'm not saying constructive criticism can't be useful to help create some awareness (step 1 in the change model) in life. However, the over-emphasis we place on the perceived weaknesses of others, such as in the case of weight and weight-loss as I've previously mentioned, is counter-productive. I want to highlight the perceived weakness in the previous statement. I believe that the stigma concerning weight is only a perception that others have. In this case, telling people that they are only beautiful or adequate once they achieve a certain body type (which in most cases is impossible, because many images are manipulated and because we are all made with different body types) has increased eating disorders. I've recently seen reports of young children (some girls as young as nine) wrap their bodies in plastic wrap, all to "fix" what society says is a weakness.

If you struggle with your self-concept—God knows I have—then I want to encourage you to use the tools in this book to totally and completely accept yourself and your body. Everything in life exists as a relationship; the most important relationship is the one you have with yourself. The better your relationship, the better the trust. The better the trust, the more willing you are to continue to commit to yourself. Think about someone in your life with whom you have a good relationship. Do you trust that person? Likely, you do. How can you continue to have a good relationship with that person and keep that trust? You invest your time (qualitative or perhaps experiential). If you don't put time into the relationship, it dies. If you don't put time into a healthy relationship with yourself, then you can't trust yourself or make the choice to live with the three P's, or develop a strong and courageous self-concept.

Relationships don't just exist with people, but in all with which we interact and experience each day. We have relationships with time, money, stress, food, happiness, purpose, momentum, change, sleep, health. The list goes on and on. If you have a negative relationship with time in which see it as a barrier, then you will likely feel rushed and make the excuse of never having enough of it. If you have a positive relationship with money, you're likely to take better care of it and invest it in things that will create appreciated returns. If you have a strong relationship with stress, which many do, then you will continue to feel stressed. All these relationships are interconnected. If you have a positive relationship with stress, meaning you consciously choose a resilient manner to overcome it (especially when appreciation, gratitude, or optimism are present), then it plays a role in the strength of your immune system is or your blood pressure (because stressful situations, when chronically considered, negatively affect both). If you have high stress, which contributes to poor health, it will likely negatively affect your emotional state on a deeper level. When you want to make a choice to eat healthfully or exercise, you are more likely to believe (belief translates into effort) that you can make those choices.

This is why I spend so much time focusing on how you view time to create more energy and momentum. The moment you stop moving forward towards your goals, dreams, and aspirations is the moment you metaphorically fall over. You were meant to do great things in this life. As you develop healthy relationships with everything in your life, you'll come to realize the value the three P's hold in helping you create and maintain momentum.

This concept is also grounded in neuroscience. Our brains are made up of billions of neurons. As you make decisions around your thoughts, feelings, logic, and intuition, you develop and build the strength of neurological connections, the relationships in your brain. And as your brain continues to strengthen the connections of our daily activities, the more subconscious your choices become. This is like taking out the trash. For me, the garbage truck comes every Monday. So, every Sunday night I put the trash out so the truck can pick it up and haul it to the dump yard. I've done this so repeatedly that I don't even have to remind myself to do it anymore. Another example is pushing the snooze button on the alarm clock. If you've built a strong neural connection that has you pressing your snooze button five times before you finally get up, then it's become an automatic and programmed decision in your brain. Our brains are hardwired to complete tasks that we do frequently and the associations intertwined in them. Take the stigma of how we associate being thin with health or beauty for example. This is a cultural neural connection one develops over time based on how one sees, lives, and operate in the world. It isn't something inherent; it is something one learns. These pathways are simply additions to our behavior, beliefs, attitudes, and thoughts—everything that we are.

Chapter 9:
Motivation

As you continue to set goals and create your ideal self, consider the different perspectives that will help keep you committed throughout your journey. One of them is motivation, which comes in two main types: intrinsic and extrinsic. Intrinsic motivation focuses on internal, subjective (qualitative) rewards such as mastery or experiential learning. For example, learning to master a task, such as learning how to run only for the purpose of mastering it, is intrinsic motivation. Learning to master IRONMAN with Katie and Adam came from within. I felt rewarded internally, because of the experience it created and all that I learned about myself throughout the process.

Extrinsic motivation focuses on external, objective (quantitative) rewards. We'll stick with running as an example. Those who focus on time (quantity) tend to be extrinsically motivated. In my case, if you can recall back to the introduction, I originally decided to run a marathon because I wanted a t-shirt and medal (both extrinsic).

Research supports that as extrinsic motivation increases, intrinsic motivation decreases. Extrinsic motivation relates to pleasures experienced outside the body and personality and is transactional in nature. Meanwhile intrinsic motivation relates to the authentic harmonizing of the mind, body and spirit, and is transformational in nature. All exist as a unique relationship which informs which choices are more attractive and satiable.

While you can have a healthy relationship with both, research supports that those who are intrinsically motivated are more likely to stay committed to their goals. That's probably why diet programs fail so often. People are worried so much about the number of pounds (extrinsic) or the weight (extrinsic when self-image and the way you want others to see you is based on societal pressures to conform). Lisle and Goldhammer present in their book, The Pleasure Trap, a model of subconscious motivation. It stems from the fact that we are born to seek pleasure, avoid pain, and take the path of least resistance (energy conservation). These are the most basic and primitive aspects of human motivation. That served us well when food was scarce and risk of bodily harm more prevalent; however, now that we have evolved as a human race to have adequate access to food and personal safety, such subconscious wiring limits our thinking and our potential. As previously mentioned, your brain and the networks within it are malleable, so new circuits and cognitive processes can be created. This is called, neuroplasticity. You can rewire and restructure your neural networks to serve your needs like transforming from a book to a ball (recall the physics analogy). All that we've discussed thus far, if implemented in your life, will create new pathways and cognitive relationships.

Here's my own version of the motivational triad, which focuses on your personal development. I call it Motivational Triad 2.0:

1. Seek happiness – I've already discussed the many benefits of happiness. Just remember, it is a result of doing things that put you in a positive emotional state. In this case, just add the three P's.

2. Optimize pain – Optimism is all about creating perspective. As I pointed out earlier, perspective is a very healthy way to deal with adverse situations in life. For me, racing with Katie and putting my body through pain helps me learn and grow (which is how I optimize it).

3. Take the path of high resistance (use and create more energy) – Recall the physics lesson earlier in the book that talked about creating more energy and momentum; that's exactly what this is. Take a step outside your comfort zone. There are tons of conscious energy and momentum in the unknown, the uncertainty, and it's waiting for you.

When it comes to doing what you believe is necessary for you to grow and create momentum in your life, and especially when working towards a life filled with positivity, passion, and purpose, remember that external influences such as people, fame, possessions, and other types of extrinsic rewards will try to get in the way of what is internally important.

People can't see what you see. They don't know what you've experienced in life, all that you've overcome, or all that you hope to be. They are only working with bits of information. So, when someone tries to point out weaknesses, just remember that trying to improve upon your weaknesses is a form of extrinsic motivation and an extremely inefficient process. Living your life to please others is not only impossible, it's fatiguing. I know this, because it's what I tried to do. I wanted people to like me. When they pointed out my weaknesses, I tried to fix those flaws to please them, not because I truly found value in it. What I finally realized was that it wasn't important to care what people thought of me; rather, it was only important to care what the right people thought of me. I limit this list to ten people such as mentors, close friends, family, whomever you trust most in life.

Let me reemphasize that once more: whomever you trust in your life most. This might mean that there are people close to you who want to tell you their opinion of yourself and what you need to change in your life to be successful. If you don't trust them, then it's likely because you don't have a good relationship with them. So why on Earth would you try to make improvements based on what they say? They are only working partial information. They don't appreciate all the uniqueness that is you. If your list is greater than ten, then I suggest removing some people. That doesn't mean you can't still have a relationship with the people who don't make your list, only that the more people you try to please, the more resistance it will add to your life. Resistance slows down your momentum, your energy, your desire to live with the three P's.

The 112-mile bike course of IRONMAN Wisconsin was one of the most physically and mentally challenging things I've ever done. I loved it. We finished the bike about thirteen minutes before the cutoff. Katie, Adam, and I knew that the hardest part of the race was over. Now, we just had to stay focused as we worked towards our goal of finishing the 26.2-mile run. As Adam pushed Katie from our transition point, we found our groove. It had been about 10.5 hours since we first started our adventure that day. To be quite honest, our legs felt great. Sure, they were tired, but we had about 6.5 hours to finish before the cutoff. That belief (remember, belief drives attitude which drives effort), that hope, fueled a fire inside us that nothing could extinguished. The thought of crossing the finish line, and creating an experience that we would carry with us for the rest of our lives flooded our emotions with positivity, passion, and purpose. Above all, it was fun. We had a blast! Everything that we had all experienced separately—success, fear, failure, pain—had brought us to this unique state of mind. We goofed off, sang songs, and lived precisely in the moment, in a state of consciousness.

What was amazing was that we attracted athletes to hang with us for different legs of the run. Mind you, we had just exerted about 30 percent more effort during the race by pulling Katie on the bike and swim, the only athletes doing such during the race. Sure, we'd used more physical energy, but the mental and spiritual energy that radiated through our team attracted other participants. Our perspective was on-point. Our nutrition was on-point: potato chips, cookies, and Coke® (which again, is not "bad," because it provided us and many athletes with fuel to continue to finish the race). The starches, fats, and sodium from the potato chips were mind-blowing, and the sugar from the cookies and Coke® was heavenly. To me, these foods were necessary at that time. (I had burned between 8,000 – 10,000 calories at that point – I'll pass on the broccoli.)

We ate. We sang. We laughed. We were alive! We drove out any and all negativity in our minds by having fun. I always enjoyed having fun growing up. I would do things that I thought created more joy and happiness. As I got older, people told me more and more that I should stop trying to have so much fun. Doing that, I felt like I lost a part of my identity. I realized that, for me, life was meant to be fun. As I continued to find and live with the three P's, I discovered that fun was, again, all in my perspective.

The motivational triad 2.0 previously discussed was how I decided to have fun. I challenged myself physically and mentally. As a result, that was my fun. Racing with Katie was fun for me. Running marathons became fun for me. I began coaching athletes who wanted to learn how to run in the winter. All this was fun for me!

I recall a time when Katie and I were attempting to raise $2500 for myTEAM TRIUMPH. We had raised about $700 and had one week left to hit our goal. I began to lose hope, since it was so close. However, I quickly realized that type of thinking was counterproductive. So, some friend and I put our heads together, and came up with an idea of running on a treadmill until we raised the rest of the money we needed to achieve our goal. To make this even more fun, we had some professors at the university I attended commit to shaving their heads if we met our fundraising goal. They were both married. Could you imagine a husband and wife with freshly shaved heads?

On the last day of fundraising I hopped on a treadmill at the local YMCA at 5:00 a.m. in the morning. The goal was to run a marathon. (Mind you, I was not yet trained for that distance.) I was extrinsically motivated to reach the financial goal ($2,500) and shave some professors' heads, but was intrinsically motivated to challenge myself and master an extremely difficult task (motivational triad 2.0). As the day progressed, and I neared $2500, which came after about five hours on the treadmill, I decided it might be worthwhile to push a bit further. I mean, why not have a bit more fun. I decided I would go 12 hours total. My legs were tired. My mind felt numb from running in place. I had posted a little picture of Katie up in front of me for some inspiration. After twelve hours of running, forty-three miles total, Katie and I raised $3,800. We beat our goal by $1,300.

The sacrifice was definitely worth the reward. Not only did we contribute more funds to myTEAM TRIUMPH, but I coordinated an event at the university to shave the two professors' heads. Many students took turns using the hair clippers to remove their hair. The chancellor of the university even took a turn. We all had fun that day! It truly put me—and I'm sure a number of others—in a positive emotional state. I found that I could still have fun in life, even if people told me not to.

I've realized that people try to point out weaknesses (being overly serious, if that's even a weakness), based on how they've lived and experienced the world. They're essentially trying to make you more like them. You don't need to be exactly like someone else. You are already an amazing, unique, and extraordinary person, just as you are. The fact that you have life in and of itself is value enough! You need to be the best (insert your name here) that you can be!

As I ran with Katie and Adam, I realized that everything about me was expanding: the way I saw the world, the way I responded to situations, the choices I made, the beliefs I had. Everything was changing all because I wanted to have a little fun and live the as the best, the one, and only Aaron Hunnel in this world. We met many people during the marathon portion of the IRONMAN. Some of the athletes really struggled. Some athletes stopped to just say hi. Some ran a few miles with Katie as a source of inspiration. As we made our way to the finishers chute, we kept our physical and mental spirits high.

Chapter 10:
The Power of Teamwork

People are the greatest gifts we have to help us succeed in life. From the moment we are born into this world until the moment we pass away, we are influenced, affected, and changed by people. Understanding this relationship is important. We all have different strengths, talents, and treasures. We all have different experiences, perspectives, and definitions of success. What sets the human race apart from other species is our ability to look beyond our differences, find our similarities, and come together to support one another. This heuristic approach to life is one of the most sustainable and productive forms of building a community or, more particularly, a team.

Teams are commonplace in all levels of society. A band, comprised of a guitar, drummer and singer, is essentially a team. An organization made up of different levels of management, departments, and leaders is essentially a team. Take a gander at what a quarterback, wide receiver, offensive line, defense, and coaching staff all have in common. You guessed it: they are all part of a team. See the pattern here? We have teams at all levels of society. You could even stretch this conceptualization of teamwork a bit further and argue that communities, territories, states, nations, continents, and even the world are one really big team. Some flourish as teams, embodied with the collective values and vision to which each member is committed. Then there are other teams which struggle, mainly because of their inability to find a way to come together.

You've probably heard this term before: "A team is only as strong as its weakest link." I believe that's wrong, because all members of a team play a viable role in each other's success. If you believe that someone is your weakest link, then you're likely to treat him or her as such. This mindset creates an unhealthy dynamic and puts a lot of pressure on the "weakest" to the point that it disrupts the team's ability to focus on their vision and values and achieve that which they (the team) want to achieve.

A more appropriate saying would be: "A team is only as strong as its ability to link." That means a team's likelihood of success depends on how well a team can gel, come together, and use the strengths of each other to create a solid foundation for success. If you focus on someone's weakness, you are likely to miss his or her strengths. Capitalizing on strengths is necessary for this "linking" to occur. Following are a couple ideas on how to and how not to bring a team together:

1. Understand the following model in terms of how they relate to group dynamics.

a. Forming – This is the initial stage in which people on the team start to learn about others on their team. Some may feel a bit anxious about meeting new people or about what others will think of them. As relationships begin to grow, the team will move to the next stage.

b. Storming – During this stage, the team starts to push the boundaries beyond a simple relationship with each other. Authority can be challenged. Conflict is likely to arise. Some may resist the direction of others. This is all part of the process. One very important piece during this stage, however, is that there be some sort of mediation and resolution. Conflict can be healthy, but only if the intent is to resolve the conflict and use it to learn and grow together. Unresolved conflict leads to various degrees of angst, turmoil, and individualism within the team, which prolongs cohesive alignment of vision, goals, and values. Once a team can effectively surmount conflict, they will gain greater insight and clarity of what they want and move into the next phase.

c. Norming – During this stage, teams resolve to respect differences and appreciate strengths. Cohesiveness becomes particularly strong, and the commitment to each other trumps the commitment to self. As this mindset and dynamic increase and improve, teams move into the final phase.

d. Performing – During this phase, teams begin to peak towards growth and commitment. Performance perpetually increases. Relationships are strong, strengths are amplified, and people are socially driven to perform with regard to the success of the team, rather than the success of the individual.

A team can move between any stages of this dynamic. This fluctuation can be healthy and empower teams to become resilient and develop processes and procedures that help them move towards performance, true performance. Many teams are stuck in the norming phase. They cannot move past this phase, because there is too much focus on self, a lack of leadership to guide the team, or criticism of others' weaknesses, rather than recognition of strengths. The most successful teams are fluid and can move between each phase with the understanding, awareness, and intention of learning, growing, and commitment.

2.   Another concept for developing strong teams is to avoid the phenomena, groupthink. While many of us focus on what we should do, we must also consider what we should not do. That's where groupthink comes in. Groupthink is an inefficient decision-making process of teams who think that they are invulnerable to poor ideas, albeit through a myriad of dynamics, most of which include members feeling that they can voice objections, alternative considerations, or unethical dilemmas. Sometimes groups develop ideas and implementations that result in disastrous courses of action. All the while, those disasters could have been avoided had team members voiced their opinions. This term, introduced by Irving Janis in the 1970s, includes eight symptoms:

a. Illusion of invulnerability: Excessive optimism

146

in the idea(s) around extreme risk-taking.

b. Collective rationalization: Avoiding clear and present warnings, and false or illogical assumptions.

c. Belief in inherent morality: Belief that the cause is noble and willful ignorance of ethical and moral consequences.

d. Stereotyped views of out-groups: Construction of negative opinions of those outside the group.

e. Direct pressure on dissenters: Castigation of those who oppose and argue ideas, stereotypes, or commitment in the group as disloyal.

f.Self-censorship: Withholding a viewpoint that contradicts a perceived group consensus.

g. Illusion of unanimity: False perception that all team members agree with the decision because some are silent or do not express dissent.

h. Mindguards: Members who protect the group from information that threatens the group's cohesiveness or complacency.

Examples of groupthink occur all the time, sometimes without our awareness. For example, tobacco companies built their industry by dismissing the dangers of tobacco use as inconclusive, which prolonged buy-in from Americans around a negative health risk. A more practical example in the workplace would be a manager enforcing a rule that prohibits employees from talking to one another while at work. This example, which falls under the pretext of "belief in inherent morality," suggests that employees will be more focused on their work if they don't socialize. Although that might seem like a noble cause to get the most out of employees while on the clock, one would quickly realize that depriving employees of the basic human psychological need to connect with others will backfire. What you would likely find is that whoever enforces that illogical system has established a dynamic wherein team members won't speak their mind for fear of retaliation (self-censorship). It also ignores input from those outside the group who provide negative, constructive feedback (stereotyped views of out-groups) on the secondary and tertiary consequences of this disastrous action. Consequently, the group becomes less productive, has greater frustration, and does not support their manager. Consequently, they fail as a team.

So how can you avoid the product of groupthink? Try the following:

1. Explicitly emphasize team members to remain impartial.

2. Encourage disagreement.

3. Assign a team member to be the "devil's advocate."

4. Ask for an outside opinion.

5. Encourage discussion outside of the meeting.

6. Ask for everyone's true opinion and value each one's input.

Teamwork is often seen as difficult because of the work it requires to bring people together. Some of us say, "All I can focus on is myself." That mindset counters any ability to facilitate group cohesiveness. The best teams are those who find a way to put their differences aside and find the similarities which bring them together. It may be challenging at first, especially if you have a dynamic that has poor, ingrained processes and procedures.

Often, the hardest things are the most rewarding. Use each other's strengths. Find each other's the best attributes. Communicate, communicate, communicate by listening first, and talking second. Above all, don't focus on your weakest link; focus on the link that will empower members of the team to rise above themselves, support the collective vision and values, and embark upon the journey as a single unit.

As we approached the finishers chute, everything turned surreal. The colors surrounding us seemed brighter, more vibrant. Christian, the executive director, asked if we wanted to walk Katie down the finishers chute. We knew that it would take more time (quantitative). Adam and I figured that this day was all about the time (experiential) spent in struggle solely for the experience: let's do it. We brought Katie's chair over to the side. The finishers chute was about 200 meters long, about the size of two American football field. The crowd cheered for all the athletes as they made their way down the chute. You could hear Mike Riley, the announcer, calling out names as athletes crossed the finish line. Lights shone all around and lit the way as we mustered up the physical and mental strength to make our way towards the finish.

A volunteer quickly came up to us and shouted

over all the background noise, "Do you think this is a good idea? This is a really long way for her to walk!"

I looked at Adam, then at Katie. She was right. It was quite a long distance for Katie to walk, especially because Adam and I would have to support her. What if she fell? What if we didn't have the physical strength to carry her? As soon as those thoughts came into my mind, I saw Katie reach out her hand and gently place it on the volunteer's shoulder. I drowned out all the noise so I could hear what Katie had to say.

"It's okay," she iterated to the volunteer. "I can do this. I can do this with my willpower."

At that very moment, all fear and doubt left me. I was now more energized and excited than ever before. I wasn't going to take the easy road now. We were going to walk Katie down that chute. Her words echoed in my mind: "I can do it with my willpower!" Adam and I both linked arms around Katie, helping to support her weight so she could move her legs. As we took each step, the crowd grew louder. Spectators took photos and videos. They shouted words of encouragement and praise. Some wept. Some smiled. Some even reached out to touch Katie to congratulate her for the effort she put into the day.

I readjusted my arm, needing a better grip underneath Katie as we finished the final twenty meters of the finishers chute.

"Come on, Katie, there's something I want to tell you!" I heard the announcer state over and over as we trudged our way to victory.

Finally, after fifteen hours and thirty-nine minutes, we crossed that finish line while simultaneously hearing over the speakers, "Katie Neuman, You are an IRONMAN!"

"Mission accomplished," I thought.

I wiped away some tears welling up in my eyes as Adam and I placed Katie back in her chair.

Katie looked up, smiled and said. "That's the furthest I've ever walked in my life."

I sat on that statement for a few miles, smiled, cried, and gave her, Adam, and our volunteers a hug. "The longest I've ever walked in my life?" I thought. "How amazing!" That statement struck an emotional nerve. I've never been the same since.

To be part of something so extraordinary with amazing people showed me exactly what life is about. We weren't meant to be these stressed human beings with not enough time and plenty of excuses to do what's important to us. Life's too valuable to waste energy on thoughts that don't serve us. Stress, anxiety, fear: these emotions experienced over long periods of time create friction and resistance and keep us from achieving our full potential.

As I reflect on this final moment of a day that changed my life forever, I realize two things:

First, people are necessary to live and grow in the world. Think about the value money would have if there were no people. Think about the value business would have if there were no people. Think about the value a sporting event would have if there were no people. Think about the value life would have there were no people. Without people, everything in the world loses value. Money, business, even life cannot exist without people, cannot exist without you. That's why it's so important that you make people—the right types of people—part of your life. People will influence your emotional state, your hobbies, your beliefs, and your choices. Don't you want those who help empower you, motivate you, and energize you to live with positivity, passion, and purpose? You become like the people with whom you keep company, so choose the right people to be part of your life.

Katie, Adam, and I had so much support throughout our IRONMAN journey, there is no way we would managed to finish without them. From the support vehicles to the cheer sections, friends, family, and volunteers alike made this transcendent experience possible.

Second, willpower is conceived in your mind. Some research suggests that willpower is a limited resource only when we believe it's a limited resource. It's argued that your ability to self–regulate (make choices that align with your goals, dreams, and desires) decreases as you make decisions throughout the day. Therefore, if your day is filled with lots of stuff, especially stuff that increases stress, results in negative emotional states, and slows momentum, then it will be more difficult for you to make choices and self-regulate based on the things you want for yourself. A simple example would be that you plan to go workout for thirty minutes after a long stressful day; but, instead, you decide to watch two hours of television and eat a bag of potato chips. Most people don't have the willpower because they don't believe (belief drives effort) they have the willpower—the more that gets used throughout the day, the less remains available. This isn't true.

Willpower is something to which you always have access. It's just a matter of whether you choose to see it as an unlimited resource. Katie slept only a couple of hours the night before IRONMAN, and, after being up for about twenty hours straight on three hours of sleep, she said, "I can do it with my willpower!" And she did. The more you see willpower as an unlimited resource (which you can use the change model to implement), the stronger the neural connection gets in your brain. And the stronger that connection gets, the better relationship you will have with making hard choices when you don't feel it's worth the time.

Katie and I have developed a wonderful bond by racing together. After IRONMAN, we decided that we enjoyed pushing ourselves beyond our perceived limits because it was fun! We've since run a 50-mile race, which raised enough money for Katie to have her very own customized racing chair. Now anyone who wants to run with her, at any time, can do so. By the time you've read this, we will have accomplished our longest experience yet. Katie, Adam, and I have teamed up once more to run one hundred miles. At the end of this race, Katie is going to walk just over one mile. It will be the longest distance she's ever walked in her life. As I train my body to run one hundred miles—which, pushing Katie, will take an estimated 24 hours—I want to share one last piece of information.

Training for an endurance event requires commitment and action. The more I commit, the more trained my muscles become, the lower my risk for injury, the better I can live with the three P's. Developing the muscles to handle intensive training has increased their resilience. It's gotten to the point at which I've run a total of eighty-one miles in a period of four days. At the end of some of these weeks, my legs feel in great shape, no soreness and only a little fatigue. The point is this, as you continue to train and expand your mind to incorporate some or all of the lessons in this book, you will find yourself more resilient, able to bounce back more quickly so you can keep the momentum going and the energy flowing. You'll feel a shift in your mindset as you start to experience the world.

Carol Dweck talks about two different mindsets that help us and hinders us in life: They are the fixed and growth mindsets. The fixed mindset operates out of fear. We compare and base our adequacy on how we measure up to other people. With the fixed mindset, you believe that success is predicated on the gifts, talents, and treasures with which you were born. It generalizes everything it encounters and works in the darkness of absolutes. For example, if you believe you fail at something, it makes you a failure.

Growth mindset relies on the effort to build skills and talent. Failing at something doesn't make you a failure, it just means that you need to try something a different way to make it work. And when you see people succeed around you, it doesn't mean that you are inadequate. It only means that they are finding what works for them. As I've continued down this path of living with a growth mindset, I often recall something that developed in my life. It wasn't always this way; but, the more I've done it, the better I've become and the more energy and momentum I get as a result. It embodies all that I am, in regards to me living with positivity, passion, and purpose.

If you can recall my experience in Boston, I gave a speech to attendees of the Patriot's Day celebration. That experience scared the crap out of me, but it also came to be something for which I found a true passion. Since Boston, I've done more and more speaking events, because I love meeting and connecting with people and using my story to inspire them to live their greatest life. It became such a passion that I started my own business so I can share my message all over the world. I would never have believed (remember, belief drives effort) that this was possible while stuck in a life of alcoholism, anger, and fixed mindset thinking. I now understand that this is what I was meant for in this life. I gain so much personal momentum and energy as a result. It is the light that takes away the darkness, the clear water that removes all the red dye. When I'm speaking, I'm alive. And to think that an experience in Boston, which pieced together in a way that I could never have planned for, put me on a trajectory to self-love, transcendence, and actualization.

A community is defined as a group of people living in the same place or having a particular characteristic in common. We seek to bring about positive, rewarding and sustained change. We can only do this once we have the awareness and understanding that we must bring our greatest resources together, the greatest resource being people.

There are many different types of communities in all aspects of life.

Is one position within the community more important than the other?

Does a single position carry more value, more significance, or more meaning?

I think not. Value rests in the relationships that we, as individuals, choose to build, cultivate, and support. It is the interweaving of our personalities, our strengths, our alignment of commitment and perseverance towards a particular value, idea, or cause. It transcends us as individuals and inspires us to relinquish our selfishness for something greater, more profound than ourselves.

Do not the segments within our communities, and the people within them, work together in a relationship with one another to accomplish the value each group determines? It is such that we must focus on building relationships with each other if we hope to create more value for our community and strengthen our cause for that which we desire to accomplish.

Those who seek power will create significant relationship gaps and vulnerabilities, and, therefore, forgo the ability to unite and form a community. Like will attract the like, and only people who seek power will support the cause. It will result in chaos and the vision, the heart, and the soul will seek transaction rather than transformation.

Consequently, the vision will surely fail, end and die. The pursuit of individualism, whether a person or organization, is the largest and most unsustainable form of life.

Ego cannot bring people together. Only the heart can do that. We should shift our focus and conversation to building connections, enhancing teamwork, and fostering relationships. This is the greatest attribute of our species and the greatest service of mankind. It reflects the selflessness of the human condition and is of the highest order of human achievement. Aim to build a community and you will attract those who share that goal. More people seeking a strong community will buy into the cause and collectively enhance the strength and power of the community. It is cyclical. It is profound.

If you bend a branch over your thigh, it will surely break. But bring branches together in a bundle and try to bend them over your thigh, and you will likely see them bend and flex, but not break. A branch alone is weak, but a bundle of branches, much like that of a community, is strong.

A community is made up of people, various groups, and organizations. Each of us brings a certain skill, a certain strength, a certain value. Our differences do not push us apart, they bring us together.

There are communities all around us. The town or city in which you live is a community. The state or territory in which you live in is a community. The country in which you live in is a community. Our world is essentially our community.

Wherever you are in the world, and whatever you do in the world, understand this: You are important. You carry value. We are stronger together than we are apart. We create more value together than we do apart. We become a total community, a world of humanity, together, not apart.

Let us commit to each other and build a strong community in our world, together, united, and strong. Your time is limited, but you are not. You are capable of extraordinary things. Your past doesn't define you, rather it refines you. It makes you better, stronger, capable of so much more.

Thank you so much for taking the time (experiential) to read this book. I hope you've learned more about yourself and developed some clarity on what you can do to live your greatest life. If you liked the content and would be interested in learning more about what I do, please visit aaronhunnel.com or connect with me on Facebook, Instagram or Twitter. As always, never forget to live with positivity, passion, and purpose. It's time to move, *Upwards*.

For daily doses of Positivity, Passion and Purpose follow Aaron on social media:

Facebook:
https://www.facebook.com/aaronhunnelauthor/
or @aaronhunnelauthor

Instagram: @aaronhunnel

Twitter: @aaronhunnel

To book Aaron for your next event, visit aaronhunnel.com.

Made in the USA
Charleston, SC
26 December 2016